GCSE

DNA

Dennis Kelly

Oxford Literature Companions

Notes and activities: Su Fielder
Series consultant: Peter Buckroyd

OXFORD
UNIVERSITY PRESS

Contents

What are Oxford Literature Companions?

Oxford Literature Companions is a series designed to provide you with comprehensive support for popular set texts. You can use the Companion alongside your play, using relevant sections during your studies or using the book as a whole for revision.

Each Companion includes detailed guidance and practical activities on:

- **Plot and Structure**
- **Context**
- **Characters**
- **Language**
- **Themes**
- **Performance**
- **Skills and Practice**

How does this book help with exam preparation?

As well as providing guidance on key areas of the play, throughout this book you will also find 'Upgrade' features. These are tips to help with your exam preparation and performance.

In addition, in the extensive **Skills and Practice** chapter, the 'Exam skills' section provides detailed guidance on areas such as how to prepare for the exam, understanding the question, planning your response and hints for what to do (or not do) in the exam.

In the **Skills and Practice** chapter there is also a bank of **Sample questions** and **Sample answers**. The **Sample answers** are marked and include annotations and a summative comment.

How does this book help with terminology?

Throughout the book, key terms are **highlighted** in the text and explained on the same page. There is also a detailed **Glossary** at the end of the book that explains, in the context of the play, all the relevant literary terms highlighted in this book.

Which edition of the play has this book used?

Quotations have been taken from the Oberon school edition of *DNA* (ISBN 978-1-84002-952-9).

How does this book work?

Each book in the Oxford Literature Companions series follows the same approach and includes the following features:

- **Key quotations** from the play
- **Key terms** explained on the page and linked to a complete glossary at the end of the book
- **Activity boxes** to help improve your understanding of the text
- **Upgrade** tips to help prepare you for your assessment

Key quotations from the play

Key terms explained on the page and at the end of the book

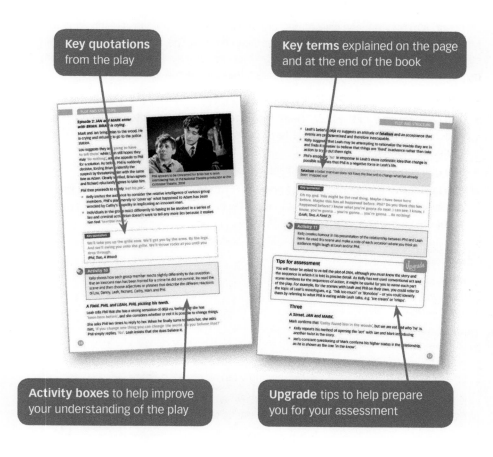

Activity boxes to help improve your understanding of the play

Upgrade tips to help prepare you for your assessment

Plot

DNA is divided into four main parts, labelled One, Two, Three, Four. Each of these parts is further split into action that takes place in three settings: in 'A Street', in 'A Field' or in 'A Wood'. In this book, the longer sequences set in 'A Wood' are further divided into shorter individual **episodes**.

The following summaries outline each of the sequences of action in *DNA*. Many of the sequences consist of characters talking about events that have happened either before the action begins or between the scenes that Kelly shows us.

While the plot of the play is relatively simple, it is the exploration of the characters' reactions to events that are the playwright's focus of interest and what you will be studying as you prepare for your assessment.

One

A Street. MARK and JAN.

Mark and Jan, two teenage classmates, are in mid-conversation. Jan is responding to Mark's shocking news that someone is dead and her first line, 'Dead?' is a powerful start to the play. Jan asks Mark if there is a 'mistake' or if it's 'a joke' or if the person might just be 'hiding'. Each time, Mark insists that the person is, in fact, 'dead'.

Jan ends the scene, in a state of alarm, asking, 'What are we going to do?'

- The opening 'line' of the play, 'Dead?' plunges the audience into a mystery which is not revealed for another two scenes. This is an aspect of Kelly's dramatic method.
- The difference between truth and lies is very important in this play.
- The last line of the section, 'What are we going to do?' introduces the state of anxiety that the young characters in this play are in, facing a situation that they do not have the maturity to deal with.

> **Key quotation**
>
> What are we going to do?
> *(Jan, One, A Street)*

Activity 1

Read the scene aloud. Notice how many times Jan asks a question, how many times Mark says 'Yes', 'Yeah' or 'No', and how Jan reacts each time.

Is this the way you and your friends converse in real life? Or do you think Kelly has crafted the dialogue artificially to create dramatic tension?

Tips for assessment

You may have to write about the opening scene and consider its dramatic impact. Think about:

- the effect of starting the play mid-conversation and with a question
- the brevity of the scene
- its abrupt ending
- the **cliff-hanger** effect of ending the play with another question.

---

cliff-hanger a tense and exciting ending to an episode

episode a section of action or dialogue between two or three actors that advances the plot of a play and drives the action forward

theme a subject or idea that is repeated or developed in a literary work

---

A Field. LEAH and PHIL, PHIL eating an ice cream.

Phil silently eats his ice cream, while Leah chatters on. She asks Phil what he is thinking, but when he ignores her, Leah launches into a long speech, made up of a series of questions and statements about her identity, her feelings and her experience of friends and fear.

Leah is concerned primarily about what Phil thinks of her, asking him, 'are you thinking a negative thing'. She wants to know if he thinks she talks too much and if she disgusts him.

> **Key quotation**
>
> So kill me, Phil, call the police, lock me up, rip out my teeth with a pair of rusty pliers, I talk too much, what a crime, what a sin, what an absolute catastrophe, stupid, evil, ridiculous
> *(Leah, One, A Field 1)*

When Phil continues to ignore Leah, she tells him, 'you're not perfect actually, Phil'.

Leah admits to being 'scared' at school, adding that she is 'not the only one' scared by 'the fear that everyone here lives in, the brutal terror'.

Phil offers no comfort as Leah tries to persuade him that they 'need each other'. When Phil fails to respond, Leah returns to her original question: 'What are you thinking?'

Jan and Mark appear, and when Mark says 'We need to talk to you', Leah senses trouble and utters a horrified, 'Oh, shit'.

- Phil's silence is one of the tools he uses to exert power over Leah. The ever-changing shifts in the relative power of group members make power a key **theme**.

- Leah refers to her 'crime' of talking too much and suggests a range of extreme punishments for herself. Later, Kelly explores the group's unwillingness to accept responsibility and/or punishment for their genuine crime.
- Leah refers to how scared she and the others are, suggesting what an unsettling place school is for them.

Key quotation

I'm scared, they scare me, this place, everyone, the fear, the fear that everyone here, and I'm not the only one, I'm not the only one, Phil, I'm just the only one saying it, the fear that everyone here lives in, the brutal terror, it scares me
(Leah, One, A Field 1)

 Activity 2

There is no indication in the text of how Phil reacts with his face and/or body to what Leah is saying. If you were directing Phil, what **non-verbal** reactions would you ask him to make to Leah's **monologue**? Explain what you would want these reactions to indicate about his feelings.

A Wood. LOU, JOHN TATE and DANNY.

John Tate, Lou and Danny are in the middle of a conversation about the predicament, the difficult situation they are in. The other members of John Tate's group arrive in small clusters, interrupting the action and changing the **group dynamic** on stage.

The wood is where all the characters meet

group dynamic the inter-relationships between a group of people, including their reactions and attitudes to one another

monologue a long speech given by a single actor with no interruption from other characters

non-verbal communication that occurs when people express their feelings or attitudes without words, using facial expressions, gestures and/or movements

Episode 1

John Tate, the leader of the group, is trying to keep his nerve and hold the group together. He insists that their situation, although 'tricky', is one that he can resolve, telling them, 'Look, haven't I looked after things before?'

Tate reminds Lou and Danny how he has transformed their lives since he joined their school, turning them into a distinctive and scary clique, protecting them from the bullies who used to terrorize them. Now, 'no one bothers you and if you want something it's yours and no one bothers you and everyone respects you and everyone's scared of you'.

Tate is annoyed to hear that Lou is scared of Richard as this poses a threat to his self-image as ultimate controller of the group. He is also irritated by Lou and Danny repeating the word 'dead', so Tate makes a new group rule to ban the word.

Danny asks, 'How can you ban a word?' Under pressure, John Tate resorts to the tactics of a bully, threatening to 'bite their face. Or something' if anyone mentions the word 'dead' again. But once he sees the resentful reactions of Lou and Danny, he tries to recover the situation.

- In *DNA*, Kelly investigates different types of leader, beginning with John Tate, who employs threats and encouragement to control the group.
- Danny's concern for his own plans to become a dentist may be interpreted as selfishness, suggesting a lack of awareness about his own role in the trouble facing the group.

> **Key quotation**
>
> Look, we have to keep together. We have to trust each other and believe in each other. I'm trying to help. I'm trying to keep things together.
> *(John Tate, One, A Wood)*

Activity 3

Write a list of four or five qualities that you believe are essential in a good leader. Rank them in order of importance.

Episode 2: *RICHARD enters, with CATHY and BRIAN, CATHY grinning, BRIAN crying.*

Unaware of Tate's ban, Richard's first line 'He's dead' provokes a confrontation between them, with John Tate threatening to 'hurt' Richard. Unlike Lou and Danny, Richard stands up to John Tate, telling him, 'You shouldn't threaten me, John', causing Tate to force each group member to declare whose side they are on. Richard, Danny, Cathy and Lou each choose to side with Tate and accept his idea to 'keep calm' and 'say nothing'.

Tate turns on Brian: **'That just leaves you, Brian. You crying little piece of filth'.** Brian stops crying and defies the consensus (group agreement), announcing, **'I think we should tell someone'.**

As John **'begins to walk towards BRIAN'**, Mark, Jan, Phil and Leah enter.

- John Tate uses two recognizable strategies of insecure leadership: the threat of violence and the method of divide and rule, deliberately dividing up the group members.
- Kelly shows contrasting attitudes to the death through the characters of Cathy, who enters **'grinning'**, and Brian, **'crying'**.
- John Tate's physical movement towards Brian may suggest a violent intention.

Key quotation

I am trying to keep everyone together. Ever since I came to this school haven't I been trying to keep everyone together? Aren't things better? For us?
(John Tate, One, A Wood)

Activity 4

Do you think that John Tate acts like somebody trying to **'keep everyone together'**, as he claims? Make one list of the things he says or does that support this statement and another list of the things that contradict it.

Episode 3: *MARK and JAN enter with LEAH and PHIL, PHIL drinking a Coke.*

John Tate admits, **'I'm finding this all quite stressful. You know that?'**

Leah tries to defend Phil over whatever John Tate may think he has done, but Tate silences her, before instructing Jan and Mark to explain what has happened.

Mark and Jan narrate the events that led up to the death of Adam, a hanger-on, from outside the group. Insisting that they were **'just having a laugh'** and that Adam was **'laughing harder than anyone'**, Mark describes the sickening progress of their bullying of Adam, starting with him eating **'dirty leaves'** and ending with him falling **'hundreds of feet into blackness'**. With the exception of Leah and Phil, all of the rest of the group were involved, to some degree, in the mental and physical abuse of Adam.

John Tate accepts that Adam is **'Dead'** and also that he is not the person to save the group from the consequences of their actions. Instead he turns to Phil and Leah, saying, **'Cathy says you're clever. So. What do we do?'**

Phil issues detailed instructions to each group member, designed to shift suspicion about their involvement in Adam's death on to a fictitious 'abductor' of Adam. The plot involves lies, theft, planting false evidence and making false statements, but the key element is to ensure that when the police find Adam's jumper in the woods, it is covered in the DNA of a stranger who cannot be linked to anyone in the group.

The group are mesmerized by Phil's ingenuity and stare at him open-mouthed. He has become their new leader.

- Leah proves her loyalty to Phil by defending him to John Tate.
- Phil's plan depends on his understanding of how the police rely on DNA evidence to solve crimes.
- Neither Phil nor Leah take an active part in Phil's scheme to pervert the course of justice.

DNA

DNA (short for deoxyribonucleic acid) is a substance that occurs in the gene part of every single cell of each living thing. It contains coded information about how each species looks and behaves. In humans, the DNA stored in our genes is completely unique to each individual and determines features such as eye colour and intelligence; it defines a person's identity.

A person's DNA is unique to them

DNA evidence

This can be extracted from minute deposits of a person's cells, found in a single hair, a flake of skin, a drop of saliva or blood, sweat, mucus or even earwax. All it takes is a few cells to identify (or rule out) a suspect with near 100% certainty.

Perverting the course of justice

The criminal offence of perverting the course of justice includes making false statements to the police and attempting to conceal 'an arrestable offence'. The punishments for someone found guilty of this offence range from a fine to a maximum of life imprisonment.

Key quotations

do not be tempted to use a bin liner you have knocking around the house as that will be a DNA nightmare
(Phil, One, A Wood)

The man picks it up, runs after you covering it in DNA and then gives it back, make sure you let him drop it in the bag
(Phil, One, A Wood)

Activity 5

Phil's ideas for the cover-up appear comprehensive and compelling to the other teenagers, but the plan is not without risk. At the end of his long speech, Phil asks, **'Any questions?'** Imagine you are one of the characters involved in Phil's plan. Write a list of your concerns either about the plan as a whole or about the role Phil has asked you to play.

A Field. LEAH and PHIL sitting.

Leah explains to Phil that, contrary to popular belief, the primate species of bonobos are humans' **'nearest relative'** rather than chimpanzees. Leah describes chimps as **'evil'**, explaining, **'They murder each other'**, whereas bonobos are the opposite, even though there is only the **'tiniest change'** in the DNA that chimps and bonobos share. Phil does not respond to this information except to take out a packet of crisps.

Leah says that any chimp that is not part of a group is liable to be killed by group members

Leah asks Phil what he would do **'if I killed myself, right here in front of you'** and she proceeds to attempt to strangle herself until she lies gasping on the ground in front of Phil, who merely *'looks on'* before he *'opens his crisps and begins to eat them'*.

Undeterred by Phil's indifference, Leah sits back next to him and resumes her monologue about bonobos and their rampant sexual appetites.

In the silence that follows her description of the apes, Leah's thoughts return to the crisis situation that the group are in, concluding, **'We're in trouble now, Phil. Don't know how this'll pan out'**.

- Leah's description of how any chimp that finds itself **'outside of a group'** is liable to be **'hounded to death'** directly relates to what the teenagers have done to Adam.
- Leah explains how DNA acts as a genetic blueprint for characteristics, including aggression and sociability, as well as physical appearance; it accounts for differences between characters like Phil and Brian, for example.
- Phil's refusal to respond to Leah can be seen as a form of psychological 'violence' as she humiliates herself to gain his attention.

Activity 6

On the Internet, find out about the intelligent and gentle nature of bonobos and
how their behaviour differs from that of chimpanzees. Consider the message you
think Kelly intends the audience to understand from Leah's comparison between
the two types of apes and prepare a short presentation on the subject.

Tips for assessment

Be prepared to write about individual characters and also about their changing
relationships with one another. It's a good idea to take stock of these relationships after
each section and make some notes. For example, how do the others feel about Brian up
to this point in the play? Find some quotations to support your ideas.

Two

A Street. JAN and MARK.

Jan's reaction to Mark's news that someone is refusing to go somewhere dominates
the dialogue. The phrase, 'He's not going' is used ten times. Jan asks if the person is
'joking' or 'insane', but Mark simply shares in her amazement at the fact that 'he's
not going'. Jan's worried line, 'What are we going to do?' ends the scene.

- Brian is not referred to by name nor does Mark explain where 'he' is refusing to
  go, contributing to the build-up of suspense.

- Jan and Mark's reaction, and their agreement that Brian might be 'off his head',
  suggests how dire the situation is.

Key quotation

He's not joking, he's not going, he's said he's not going, I said you've gotta
go, he said he's not going, 'I'm not going' he said.
(Mark, Two, A Street)

Activity 7

As this episode offers no details about who Jan and Mark are talking about or where the individual is refusing to go to, the audience begins to speculate. Might they be talking about anyone other than Brian and anywhere other than the police station? Look back over the first part of the play and make a list of possible alternative scenarios being described here.

A Field. PHIL and LEAH, PHIL slowly eating a pack of Starburst...

Leah contemplates the nature of happiness before considering global warming, concluding that, in the solar system, **'It's life that upsets the natural order'**.

She asks Phil if he remembers his **'happiest moment'**, telling him that hers was sharing a special sunset with him **'Week last Tuesday'**, but still Phil *'says nothing'*.

Leah opens a Tupperware box to reveal what remains of Jerry, a pet she has killed. She asks Phil, **'Why do you think I did that?'**, but he can only shrug.

Leah suggests that since Adam's death the group are happier: **'Maybe it's just having something to work towards. Together'**.

Finally, Leah appears to show some remorse, perhaps wishing they had not done what they have done, by asking, **'What have we done, Phil?'** At that moment, Jan and Mark arrive, insisting, **'We need to talk'**.

Leah reveals the shocking news that she killed her pet, Jerry

- Leah's musings on the nature of happiness combined with her assertion that **'grief is making them happy'** invites the audience to consider what happiness means to them.

- Leah's motiveless killing of her pet, Jerry, appears shocking and out of character for Leah.

Key quotation

It's Jerry. I killed him. I took him out of his cage, I put the point of a screwdriver on his head and I hit it with a hammer. Why do you think I did that?
(Leah, Two, A Field 1)

Activity 8

Why do you think Leah killed her pet? Consider the possible reasons for her destroying Jerry and write a paragraph to support your ideas.

A Wood. PHIL and LEAH, LOU and DANNY. PHIL has a muffin.

Episode 1

News that the police are questioning a suspect about Adam's disappearance stuns Leah.

Cathy enters excitedly and appears unaware of the consequences of the arrest of an innocent man. Richard's revelation that the police have DNA evidence from the suspect 'linking him to the crime' puzzles the rest of the group.

Cathy claims that she 'showed initiative' in seeking out a postman who fitted the description Brian had given to the police. Horrified at Cathy's stupidity, the group realize that, having framed an innocent man, they could all go to prison. Leah concludes that they're 'screwed'.

* Kelly presents Cathy as the least intelligent of the group. By using her 'initiative' and not following Phil's instructions, she has further incriminated the group, pointing the blame at them.

* Kelly invites the audience to reflect on the consequences of lies and attempted cover-ups.

> **Key quotation**
>
> Well, we thought, you know, I mean you'd given a description so we thought, well, I thought, you know, show initiative, we'll look for a fat balding postman with bad teeth.
> *(Cathy, Two, A Wood)*

Activity 9

Based on the play so far, make a list of the characters. Rank them in order from the character you think is most intelligent to the one you think is least intelligent. Include your reasons for your ranking, with evidence from the text.

Episode 2: *JAN and MARK enter with BRIAN. BRIAN is crying.*

Mark and Jan bring Brian to the wood. He is crying and refusing to go to the police station.

Lou suggests they are 'going to have to tell them' while Leah still hopes they may 'do nothing', and she appeals to Phil for a solution. As before, Phil is suddenly decisive, forcing Brian to identify the suspect by threatening him with the same fate as Adam. Clearly terrified, Brian agrees and Richard reluctantly agrees to take him.

Phil appears to be concerned for Brian but is soon intimidating him, in the National Theatre production at the Cottesloe Theatre, 2008

Phil then proceeds to calmly 'eat his pie'.

- Kelly invites the audience to consider the relative intelligence of various group members. Phil's plan merely to 'cover up' what happened to Adam has been wrecked by Cathy's stupidity in implicating an innocent man.

- Individuals in the group react differently to having to be involved in a series of lies and criminal acts. Brian doesn't want to tell any more lies because it makes him feel 'terrible inside'.

Key quotation

We'll take you up the grille now. We'll get you by the arms. By the legs. And we'll swing you onto the grille. We'll throw rocks at you until you drop through.
(Phil, Two, A Wood)

Activity 10

Kelly shows how each group member reacts slightly differently to the revelation that an innocent man has been framed for a crime he did not commit. Re-read the scene and then choose adjectives or phrases that describe the different reactions of Lou, Danny, Leah, Richard, Cathy, Mark and Phil.

A Field. PHIL and LEAH, PHIL picking his teeth.

Leah tells Phil that she has a strong sensation of déjà vu, feeling that she has 'been here before', and she considers whether or not it is possible to change things.

She asks Phil ten times to reply to her. When he finally turns towards her, she asks him, 'If you change one thing you can change the world. Do you believe that?' Phil simply replies, 'No'. Leah insists that she does believe it.

- Leah's belief in déjà vu suggests an attitude of **fatalism** and an acceptance that events are predetermined and therefore inescapable.

- Kelly suggests that Leah may be attempting to rationalize the trouble they are in and finds it is easier to believe that things are 'fixed' in advance rather than take action to try to put them right.

- Phil's emphatic 'No' in response to Leah's more optimistic idea that change is possible suggests that Phil is a negative force in Leah's life.

fatalism a belief that man does not have the free will to change what has already been 'mapped out'

Key quotation

Oh my god. This might be the real thing. Maybe I have been here before. Maybe this has all happened before. Phil? Do you think this has happened before? I know what you're gonna do next. I can see, I know, I know, you're gonna… you're gonna… you're gonna… do nothing!
(Leah, Two, A Field 2)

Activity 11

Kelly creates humour in his presentation of the relationship between Phil and Leah here. Re-read this scene and make a note of each occasion where you think an audience might laugh at Leah and/or Phil.

Tips for assessment

You will never be asked to re-tell the plot of *DNA*, although you must know the story and the sequence in which it is told in precise detail. As Kelly has not used conventional act and scene numbers for the sequences of action, it might be useful for you to name each part of the play. For example, for the scenes with Leah and Phil on their own, you could refer to the topic of Leah's monologues, e.g. 'Talk too much' or 'Bonobos' – or you could identify them by referring to what Phil is eating while Leah talks, e.g. 'ice cream' or 'crisps'.

Three

A Street. JAN and MARK.

Mark confirms that 'Cathy found him in the woods', but we are not told who 'he' is.

- Kelly repeats his method of opening the 'act' with Jan and Mark introducing another twist in the story.

- Jan's constant questioning of Mark confirms his higher status in the relationship, as he is shown as the one 'in the know'.

> **Key quotation**
>
> JAN: And are you... is this... I mean are you... there's no mistake or...
> MARK: No.
> JAN: Because this is
> MARK: That's what I'm saying
> JAN: this is really
> MARK: Yeah, yes, yeah.
> JAN: really, really
> MARK: Exactly.
> *(Three, A Street)*

Activity 12

Re-read the key quotation above and consider what Kelly aims to convey about Mark's news. Write a paragraph to explain the effect of this exchange of half sentences and partially formed thoughts.

A Field. PHIL sits with a bag.

While Phil sits alone, preparing his waffle, Leah arrives, carrying a suitcase. She announces that she is 'running away'. She asks and answers a series of questions, beginning, 'Where'm I going? I dunno'.

Leah tells Phil not to try to stop her. Realizing that he seems to care only about his waffle and not about her, she drops her suitcase, admitting 'I admire you so much'. Leah credits Phil with having made everyone in school happy but she also notes that 'it's not all roses', explaining how Brian is on medication for a mental illness, 'John Tate hasn't been seen in weeks' and there's an innocent postman facing life in prison.

Leah concludes, sarcastically, 'but, you know, omelettes and eggs, as long as you've your waffle, who cares', then immediately returns to her doting dependence on Phil, asking him, 'How do you feel?'

Jan and Mark enter and demand that Leah and Phil 'come with us'.

- Kelly explores the different reactions of each group member to the events that have spun out of their control.
- Leah is suffering some sort of crisis that means that she wants to escape from an intolerable situation.
- Phil is outwardly untouched by events despite being the 'mastermind' of a criminal plot that has apparently destroyed both Brian and John Tate.

> **Key quotation**
>
> It's a big world, Phil, a lot bigger than you, it's a lot bigger than you and me, a lot bigger than all this, these people, sitting here, a lot bigger, a lot lot bigger.
>
> *Pause. PHIL starts to butter his waffle.*
>
> Don't. No words. There's no point, so... What's the point?
>
> 'Why are you going, is it me, is it us, is it what we've done, is it what we're becoming, why Leah, why, is it me, is it the impossibility of ever saying exactly what you mean?'
>
> *(Leah, Three, A Field 1)*

Activity 13

Re-read Leah's speech in the key quotation above. Do you think Leah wants to escape the aftermath of Adam's death or to free herself from her one-sided relationship with Phil? Prepare your case for a debate about this.

A Wood. CATHY, BRIAN, PHIL, LEAH, MARK, LOU and JAN.

Episode 1

Cathy and Brian have discovered Adam, traumatized, living rough in a hedge. Cathy explains how she 'threatened to gouge one of his eyes out' to make him come out of his hideout. Adam haltingly describes how he survived his fall. The group are at a loss about how to escape the consequences of their actions; as Leah says, 'I don't know how we're gonna get out of this one'.

Phil assumes control. He asks Adam if he wants to 'come back'. Adam is too dazed and confused to give a rational answer. Phil instructs Brian to lead Adam back to his hedge.

- Adam's reappearance is a real shock to the group and to the audience.
- Kelly shows how the crisis in their young lives has affected Brian and Cathy differently: while Brian has become weak-minded, Cathy has become violent.
- Adam has had an 'out-of-body experience' and believes he has been 'reborn'.

> **Key quotation**
>
> Okay. Now things are strange. Things are really, really strange, Phil. I mean with the greatest of respect, Adam, you are supposed to be dead.
> *(Leah, Three, A Wood)*

Activity 14

Adam's reappearance should be a cause for relief, even celebration. Why does the group react so negatively to his discovery? Write a paragraph to explain your ideas.

Episode 2: *BRIAN takes ADAM off. They all stare at PHIL.*

Phil takes charge, telling Mark, Jan and Lou to 'Go back home' and say nothing. He reassures Lou, 'Everything is going to be fine', but Leah protests, urging Phil to recognize that Adam is 'insane' and 'needs help'. Phil ignores Leah's objections, stating, 'If he comes back our lives are ruined' and telling Cathy, 'He can't come back'.

Using Brian as his 'guinea pig', Phil shows Cathy how to suffocate Adam with a plastic bag.

- Adam's 'first death' was violent, but accidental; his 'second death' is a pre-meditated and cold-blooded murder. Kelly shows how the group have lost all sense of conscience under Phil's leadership.

- Phil exploits Brian's mental disorder and Cathy's lack of empathy (ability to understand and share someone else's feelings) to solve the problem of Adam's reappearance and protect the group.

> **Key quotation**
>
> I'm in charge. Everyone is happier. What's more important; one person or everyone?
> *(Phil, Three, A Wood)*

Activity 15

This quotation is central to the whole of the play. Do you find Phil's argument persuasive? Write a paragraph either supporting or challenging Phil's view that the good of the group comes before the life of an individual.

A Field. PHIL and LEAH, sitting.

In *'Complete silence'*, Phil offers a sweet to Leah, who takes it and begins to cry. Phil puts his arm around Leah. She spits the sweet out before storming off. Phil calls after her.

- In this play, what is not said is often as important as what is said.

Activity 16

Make a list of possible reasons why Leah rejects Phil, then share your ideas with the rest of the class.

Tips for assessment

Be prepared to write about the way Kelly uses silence, pauses, 'beats' and unfinished sentences to convey his ideas to the audience. For example, Leah's total silence in this scene is as meaningful as any of her other speeches in the field scenes.

Four

A Street. JAN and MARK.

Jan quizzes Mark about his latest piece of news that someone is 'Gone?' Mark reveals that the rumour is that Leah has 'Moved schools' and 'Without saying a thing'.

- Jan's question, 'Does Phil know?', is the first time the pair appear not to be concerned about simply saving themselves.
- The fact that Leah has gone 'Without saying a thing' suggests that she has taken drastic action to escape Phil and the group.

A Field. RICHARD sits with PHIL.

Leah's place has been taken by Richard.

Phil is described as *'not eating'*. He is unresponsive as Richard tries to attract his attention by walking on his hands. Richard tells Phil that everyone is asking about him, wanting to know when Phil will 'come down from that stupid field?'

Phil simply ignores Richard's questions as well as the disturbing news that Richard shares about the rest of the group.

In the silence, Richard reveals that he has just had a strange experience where he felt he was 'inside a cloud' and had a revelation about 'life on other planets'.

The play ends with a final plea from Richard for Phil to 'Come back', but that is met with no answer and the pair sit 'in silence'.

- Phil has possibly suffered some sort of breakdown of his own. He is more withdrawn than before and is not eating his customary snacks.
- Kelly may be suggesting that Phil has suffered a massive delayed reaction to Adam's death or is suffering over Leah's 'desertion' of him.

Key quotation

And in that second, Phil, I knew that there was life on other planets. *(Richard, Four, A Field)*

 Activity 17

Richard is not the only character in the play to experience an **epiphany**. Make a list of all the characters who have been radically changed by their involvement in the 'Adam' incidents and make a note of how this change has shown itself in their words, action or reported behaviour.

---

epiphany a moment when someone suddenly sees or understands something in a new or very clear way

Structure

External structure

The **external structure** – or physical shape – of any piece of literature is determined by the way its content is arranged and presented by the writer. Novelists use chapters, poets use stanzas, or verses, and dramatists conventionally use acts and scenes to divide a large amount of material into shorter segments.

Modern western theatre originated in ancient Greece, where all tragic dramatists structured their plays in a similar way, by alternating sections called **choric odes** with sections of action or **dialogue** between a pair or a trio of characters called episodes. Kelly's structure owes something to this tradition. **Chorus** figures have been used by playwrights to communicate with the audience since theatre began. Modern playwrights have adapted the choric role to suit their subject matter and dramatic style. Kelly does this using the characters, Jan and Mark, to act as Chorus figures.

It was the Romans who introduced the convention of organizing their plays into acts and scenes, and this became the traditional method of structuring drama for hundreds of years. Kelly does not use the terms 'acts' and 'scenes'. Instead, he calls the four major sections of action in the play 'One', 'Two', 'Three' and 'Four'. He divides up the action within these longer sections using three asterisks (***) rather than formal scene divisions. These shorter sequences of action are labelled according to the setting they take place in: 'A Street', 'A Field' or 'A Wood'.

In parts One, Two and Three there are four sub-sections, which take place in different settings. In each major section, the sub-sections take place in exactly the same order: Street, Field, Wood, Field. The final part Four has only two sub-divisions, which take place in the Street and the Field.

Plot and sub-plot

The **internal structure** of a play relates to the organization of the story it tells. It relates to the ordering and development of the content or narrative rather than to its physical shape.

One feature of *DNA's* internal structure is its division into a main plot and a **sub-plot**. The main plot of the play covers the revelation of the 'death' of Adam and the group's reaction to it, including Phil's strategies for covering up the death and then for dealing with Adam's inconvenient reappearance. The sub-plot explores Phil's relationship with Leah. The sub-plot occurs in the scenes set in 'A Field'.

Although Phil says very little, he is the central character in the play and, like Leah, appears in both the main and the sub-plot. The scenes where Jan and Mark appear together serve the same purpose as Chorus scenes in Greek tragedy.

Activity 18

Search online for a definition of the Greek 'tragic hero' and pick out some of the features you think might apply to Phil's character and to his 'journey' through *DNA*.

Five stages

The play, as a whole, follows a somewhat compressed internal structure common to almost all drama, consisting of five stages, known as: **exposition**, development, **complication** or **reversal**, **climax**, and **denouement**.

choric ode in ancient Greek theatre, a section of text delivered by the Chorus directly to the audience

Chorus a group in a Greek tragedy that commented in unison on the action of the play

climax the highest or most intense part of a literary work

complication or **reversal** the part of a literary work that occurs when the main character's progress is complicated, reversed or threatened

denouement the resolution of the plot of a literary work

dialogue speech between any number of characters

exposition the part of a literary work that gives key information about the setting, characters and situation to help the audience make sense of it

external structure the way a piece of literature is divided into sections

internal structure the way the story in a piece of literature is organized in order to develop the narrative

sub-plot is related to, but not as important as, the main plot in fiction or drama

Writing about structure

Make sure that you know and understand the specialist vocabulary associated with the conventions of drama. By using it correctly and authoritatively, you will be able to express yourself more concisely and effectively.

You may be asked to comment on the play's dramatic structure – on the ordering of events and the dramatic effects Kelly creates through placing one particular sequence of action next to another. You might mention, for example, that the final section Four has only two sub-sections rather than four and that the scene set in 'A Wood' is not included in Four because the group that used to meet in the wood has effectively disintegrated following the murder of Adam.

Activity 19

Use the table on pages 24–25 to help you identify the episodes that correspond to the five different stages of the play's internal structure: exposition, development, complication/reversal, climax and denouement.

Part	A Street	A Field	A Wood
One, A Street	**Jan and Mark** 'Dead?' Someone is dead and it isn't a joke.		
One, A Field 1		**Phil and Leah** Phil eats an ice cream. Leah wants to know how Phil feels about her; she talks about friendship. Leah confesses to being 'scared'. **Jan and Mark** enter: 'We need to talk to you'.	
One, A Wood			**Lou, John Tate and Danny** 'screwed' John Tate tries to assure Lou and Danny that everything is 'fine' and bans the word 'dead'. **Richard, Cathy and Brian** arrive, and there is friction between Richard and John Tate. **Mark and Jan** arrive with **Leah and Phil**. They describe the torture of Adam and Mark describes him falling into the grille. Phil concocts his plan, drinks his Coke and assumes command of the group.
One, A Field 2		**Phil and Leah** Leah compares bonobos and chimps. Phil eats crisps. Leah strangles herself. 'Trouble now'	
Two, A Street	**Jan and Mark** 'He's not going'		
Two, A Field 1		**Phil and Leah** Phil eats Starbursts. Leah discusses happiness and shows Phil the remains of Jerry. **Mark and Jan** enter: 'We need to talk'.	

Two, A Wood			**Phil, Leah, Lou and Danny** *'PHIL has a muffin'* *'They've found the man'* **Richard and Cathy** enter. She's used her **'initiative'** to frame an innocent man. **Jan and Mark** arrive with **Brian**, crying. Phil threatens to kill Brian unless he identifies the man. Brian agrees and Phil eats his snack.
Two, A Field 2		**Phil and Leah** Phil picks his teeth. Leah has déjà vu. Leah believes in change, while Phil does not.	
Three, A Street	**Jan and Mark** **'Cathy found him in the woods?'**		
Three, A Field 1		**Phil** prepares his waffle. **Leah** turns up with suitcase: **'I'm running away'** even though **'Everyone's happy'**. **Jan and Mark** enter: **'You really, really better come with us'**.	
Three, A Wood			**Cathy, Brian, Leah, Mark, Lou, Jan and Phil with Adam** Adam describes how he has been living in a hedge since his ordeal. He has no memory. Phil orders Adam's execution by Cathy and Brian. Leah tries to stop them, but Phil *'just walks away'*.
Three, A Field 2		**Phil and Leah** Leah is crying. Phil offers her a Starburst, she spits it out and storms off. **'Leah? Leah?'**	
Four, A Street	**Jan and Mark** 'she's gone?'		
Four, A Field		**Richard** sits with **Phil**, who *'is not eating'*. He begs him to return to the group, **'Come back to us'**. Richard describes an epiphany about life on other planets. Phil appears completely withdrawn.	

Biography of Dennis Kelly

- Dennis Kelly was born in London in 1970.

- His breakthrough into professional theatre was with a play called *Debris*, which premiered at Theatre 503 in 2003. Then followed a string of successful productions including *Osama the Hero* (2004), *After the End* (2005), *Love and Money* (2006) and *Taking Care of Baby* (2007).

- In 2005, Kelly was commissioned to write a play for the National Theatre Connections Festival, which showcases plays written especially for and about young people of 13–19 years old. That play was *DNA*, which was included in the 2007 Festival and was subsequently produced by the National Theatre with a professional cast in 2008.

Dennis Kelly was commissioned in 2005 to write a play for teenagers, which was first performed, as *DNA*, in 2007

- Kelly has also been a successful writer for TV. In 2006 his sit-com *Pulling*, co-written with Sharon Horgan, got its first airing on BBC 3. He also wrote the script for Channel 4's dystopian series *Utopia*, screened in 2014, which contrary to its title featured the opposite of a perfect society.

- In 2012, Kelly won the Olivier Award for the best new musical with his adaptation of Roald Dahl's *Matilda*.

- Most of Kelly's work for the stage looks at contemporary society, where he explores dark themes and issues facing, for the most part, ordinary people caught up in difficult situations.

Activity 1

Search the Internet for outlines of some of Kelly's other stage plays. Can you see similarities between the issues presented in his earlier or later work and the issues presented in *DNA*? Write a paragraph about Kelly's subject matter as you understand it from your research.

Theatre in the first decade of the 21st century

At the beginning of the 21st century, 'new writing', in a variety of theatrical styles, accounted for a significant proportion of the plays produced.

Physical theatre, as practised by theatre groups such as Frantic Assembly and Gecko, continued to grow in popularity. **Story-telling theatre** groups such as Kneehigh and Theatre Alibi delighted audiences of all ages with their re-telling of folk tales, myths and popular stories using the full range of theatrical possibilities.

Verbatim theatre, from companies such as Out of Joint, Tricycle Theatre and Recorded Delivery, also rose to prominence and writers have used this style to engage directly with specific social and political issues.

Contemporary, cutting-edge playwrights were also using more conventional, **naturalistic** dramatic methods, but in experimental ways, to engage with contemporary events and issues and to speak relevantly to their audiences about the world around them.

Many of these cutting-edge playwrights, like Kelly in *DNA*, experimented with the theatrical structure of their plays. They also experimented with dramatic language, avoiding the lengthy, grammatically correct speeches that characters in more traditional drama use and achieving a **colloquial** form of dialogue closer to everyday conversation. Many playwrights use slang words, dialect and even swear words as part of a dialogue to reflect modern language use.

> **colloquial speech** conversational language
>
> **naturalism** a style of theatre that attempts to mirror real life
>
> **physical theatre** a style of theatre that places as much emphasis on the movement of the actors as on the delivery of text
>
> **story-telling theatre** a type of theatre that concentrates on telling a story, such as a fairy tale, myth or legend, using imaginative dramatic devices, such as actors playing multiple roles, puppetry and multi-media presentations
>
> **verbatim theatre** a form of theatre created by editing the spoken words or written testimony of real people about a particular event

Creating their own characters (rather than re-inventing characters from myth or legend), and using speech and action (rather than movement, story-telling devices or verbatim techniques), these playwrights mirrored contemporary society, creating a recognizably 21st century context in which their characters' 'lives' unfolded.

Many contemporary writers have focused on the experiences of young people in particular. Young playwrights like Polly Stenham (*That Face* and *Tusk, Tusk*), as well as more established writers including Simon Stephens (*Punk Rock*) and Philip Ridley (*Sparkleshark*), have written successful drama about issues that affect young people such as identity, inequality, race, gender, prejudice, crime, poverty and violence.

Activity 2

Find out what you can from the Internet about the subject matter of the plays mentioned above. Make a list of the plays that most appeal to you and try to find a copy to read for yourself.

National Theatre Connections

Connections is the National Theatre's nationwide festival of youth theatre. Each year, the Connections team invites youth theatres and school theatre groups to stage short new plays commissioned from some of the most influential playwrights of their generation.

Each amateur youth group that signs up to Connections chooses one of these plays to present in a local professional theatre. Ten of these companies then showcase their work at the National Theatre in London.

DNA was one of the most popular plays performed in the 2007 Festival. In 2008, the National Theatre mounted a professional production of it, alongside two other Festival favourites, *The Miracle* by Lin Coghlan and *Baby Girl* by Roy Williams.

Broad historical context

Although Kelly does not refer explicitly to particular events in the wider world beyond the characters' experience in *DNA*, it is interesting to consider some of the turbulent events, including natural disasters as well as 'man-made' catastrophes, that made the first six years of the 21st century highly memorable.

There was a dramatic rise in terrorist attacks, including the notorious 9/11 attacks on the USA by al-Qaeda in 2001, the Chechen storming of a Moscow theatre in 2002 and the al-Qaeda-inspired London bombings of 2005.

In 2004, a huge tsunami caused death and devastation across the Indian Ocean coastline, killing an estimated 230,000 people. A year later, Hurricane Katrina struck the Gulf Coast of the United States, causing more than $100 billion worth of damage as well as huge loss of life.

The United States and NATO invaded Afghanistan in 2001 and the offensive against Iraq began in 2003.

Scientific advances and discoveries in the early 21st century

More directly relevant to the content of *DNA* are some of the scientific developments that made the news in the run-up to the period when Kelly wrote this play.

In April 2003, the Human Genome Project was completed. This was an international scientific research project with the goal of determining the sequence of the building blocks that make up human DNA and of identifying and mapping all of the genes in one cell of a human (the genome). Kelly places DNA science at the core of his plot.

Also in 2003, a high-profile historic murder case made the headlines when it was solved using DNA evidence. Three innocent men had been jailed in 1990 for killing 20-year-old Lynette White in Cardiff. The **circumstantial evidence** that convicted them had actually been invented by people claiming to be witnesses. The convicted men were later freed and, 15 years later, using the advances in DNA technology, the real killer was identified from a blood stain on a skirting board. He confessed to the murder and was sent to prison for life.

Kelly's teen characters fabricate evidence and allow an innocent man to go to prison to cover their own tracks.

circumstantial evidence evidence that suggests that someone might be guilty but which is not conclusive

In 2005, the Kyoto international climate change agreement came into force, committing industrialized nations to reduce greenhouse gas emissions, which cause global warming. Leah refers to global warming as 'a nightmare' in the 'happiness' section *(Two, A Field 1)*.

In the same speech, Leah talks about the planet Venus and about Titan. In 2004, Venus was in the news, as it passed directly between the Earth and the Sun, appearing as a black dot travelling across the Sun's disk in an incredibly rare event known as a 'transit of Venus'.

The transit of Venus on 8 June 2004, which previously occurred in 1882

The European Space Agency launched the Venus Express in November 2005 to conduct atmospheric studies, mapping Venusian surface temperatures and confirming the planet's composition of mainly carbon dioxide, which Leah refers to in the same speech.

Data received from NASA's newly launched Cassini-Huygens spacecraft in 2004 revealed that Titan has lakes and seas of liquid methane and ethane. The space mission also provided evidence that Titan is hiding an internal, liquid ocean beneath its surface, likely composed of water and ammonia. Leah refers to this as 'oceans of liquid nitrogen' *(Two, A Field 1)*.

Popular nature programmes on TV, at the time, such as David Attenborough's *Wildlife on One* and Charlotte Uhlenbroek's *Cousins,* which covered the relationship between humans, chimps and bonobos, may have been the inspiration for Leah's 'bonobo' monologue in part One.

Activity 3

What do you think Kelly is trying to tell us about Leah's character through her chosen topics of 'conversation'? Write a paragraph based on her monologue in this section.

Geographical context: the play's setting

Kelly has commented, in interviews, that he chose not to locate *DNA* in a precise geographical setting or to write the dialogue in any particular local dialect so as to allow performers, from all over the country and across all social and ethnic backgrounds, to be able to access the play for the Connections Festival. So, although we assume that the group of teenagers in the play all go to the same school, we are not told either the type of school or where it is.

Street, field and wood

All the action is set outdoors and the action shifts between 'A Street', 'A Field' and 'A Wood'. Each of the outdoor settings is distinctive and provides the backdrop to different kinds of interaction and each is related to specific characters.

We only ever see Mark and Jan, as a pair, in the street and we don't see any of the other characters in this setting. Streets are usually busy public places where people journey to and from home, work, school or the shops. Traditionally, streets are where young people 'hang about', away from school and home. For Jan and Mark, the street is the place where they gossip about events that directly affect their group of friends.

Phil and Leah are only ever seen alone together in a field, away from the rest of the group. In some **classical** and **Renaissance literature**, it was a convention to present fields as an idyllic retreat from the hustle and bustle of city life, and to depict shepherds and shepherdesses, living in their pastoral setting, as perfectly contented with the simplicity of their lives. It may be a little far-fetched to assume

that Kelly intended to echo this pastoral tradition here. However, key features of **pastoral literature**, such as the theme of retreat and return (from real life and back to real life) and the private interaction between a 'lad' and a 'lass', do seem relevant to this private meeting place of Phil and Leah's. At the end of each of the field scenes, the arrival of Jan and Mark summons the pair back to the reality of their everyday lives.

It may be that the field offers Phil and Leah some sort of idyllic retreat from the reality of their lives

classical literature literature from ancient Greece and Rome

pastoral literature literature that presents an idealized image of country life, lived among the fields; it often involves characters retreating into the world of the countryside and then returning to their everyday lives

Renaissance literature literature in Europe written between the 14th and 16th centuries

The other scenes take place in a wood, which acts as a headquarters for the group. It is their special territory and outsiders are not welcome. John Tate makes this clear in his only scene, when, talking about other students at the school, he asks, **'Doesn't everyone want to be us, come here in the woods?'** *(One, A Wood)*.

Woods and forests have always featured in legend and literature as very special places. Traditionally, woodland has offered shelter or sanctuary to those needing to hide themselves from society. In the Robin Hood stories, for example, the woodland was home to Robin and his 'merrie men'. Robin led his band of 'outlaws' from their settlement in Sherwood Forest against the 'wicked' Sherriff of Nottingham. Shakespeare also included woods or forests in several of his plays as the settings for fugitives, outcasts and runaways.

In *DNA*, the wood provides a hideout for the teenage 'outlaws', away from the prying eyes of parents, teachers and the police.

Dennis Kelly's settings are not arbitrary ones, i.e. they are not randomly chosen. Each one has been specifically chosen to match the characters who meet there and the action that takes place there.

Activity 4

Write a paragraph on each of the three settings in the play to explain why you think it is appropriate for the characters who appear in it and the action that takes place.

Tips for assessment

Remember that all types of literature owe a debt to a long literary heritage and it is never irrelevant to consider previous literary forms that may have influenced the writer of your set text. Just make sure that you only refer to relevant influences.

Wider landscape of the play

Adam's ordeal may have begun in the woods, with him eating **'some leaves'** *(One, A Wood)*, but it is soon removed to areas that the audience never see and have to imagine. Adam is forced to nick **'some vodka'**, possibly from the Asda store, near **'the south entrance'** to the woods *(One, A Wood)*. He is then made to run across **'the motorway'** *(One, A Wood)*. Next, the group takes him **'up the grille'**, described as a **'shaft up there on the hill'** *(One, A Wood)*.

Other locations are also mentioned:

- Cathy, Danny and Mark have to break into **'Adam's house'** *(One, A Wood)*.
- Richard has to take Brian **'to the Head'** *(One, A Wood)*.

- Phil refers to both a south and an 'east entrance' to the woods and also to meeting up at 'the bridge' to 'a quiet street' and 'a charity shop' *(One, A Wood)*.

- In Two, Richard and Cathy arrive, direct from 'the police station', and Cathy has been to 'the sorting office', looking for an overweight postman to frame *(Two, A Wood)*.

- When Adam makes his surprise appearance in the play, we hear that he has been 'living in a hedge', which is 'up the hill' *(Three, A Wood)*.

- Later, Leah has 'Moved schools' *(Four, A Street)*, Danny has work experience at 'a dentist's' and John Tate is seen at the 'shopping centre' *(Four, A Field)*.

Through these references to places that we do not see, Kelly creates the outline of a believable physical context for the play.

Activity 5

Produce a map showing the locations mentioned above and on page 31. Think about how close these locations are to one another and to the school, and support your ideas with evidence from the text.

Cultural context: religion and science

Although Kelly does not dictate how the roles are cast, in terms of gender or ethnicity, the action of *DNA* unfolds in a Christian context. The teenagers frequently exclaim 'God' *(One, A Street)* or 'Jesus Christ' *(Two, A Wood)* when they are panicking or afraid, suggesting that they inhabit a loosely Christian environment. Other religious references include mention of the memorial service held for Adam, Leah's description of Phil as a 'miracle worker' *(Three, A Field 1)*, John Tate's epiphany when he 'finds' God, and his quest for forgiveness when he joins the 'Jesus Army' *(Four, A Field)*.

At the same time, Leah's discussion about bonobos and chimps suggests that, in common with most people in the 21st century, she understands the place of science in the evolution of humans and our relationship with the wider universe.

Social context: bullying

As bullying in schools has become a common, modern phenomenon, psychology experts have identified seven different types of school bully, as follows:

- **Confident bully:** appears to be strong with a sense of superiority towards others; has an inflated sense of own importance, a tendency towards violence and no empathy.

- **Social bully:** uses gossip, name-calling, teasing and exclusion to make victims feel worthless; jealous of others, with low self-esteem, hidden behind an exaggerated self-confidence.

- **Fully armoured bully**: wears 'armour' of indifference to protect the self; has a cold and emotionless exterior; real feelings are deeply buried; ruthless; can also appear charming to get own way.

- **Hyperactive bully:** often suffers from some form of learning disability; can't accurately process classmates' social cues.

- **Bullied bully:** generally a victim of bullies, who picks on weaker classmates.

The bullies in *DNA* have various ways of intimidating or controlling others

- **Bunch of bullies:** a group of potentially 'nice' kids who, collectively, do vicious acts that they would not do individually; they succumb to 'herd mentality'.

- **Gang of bullies:** a group of allies, not friends, banded together for reasons of power, control and domination over a particular area or 'turf'.

Activity 6

Use the profiles above and on page 32 to compile a list of the different types of bully in the play.

Writing about context

It is important that you don't simply force contextual information into your assessment. Instead, you should use relevant information to support and develop your ideas.

Some contexts that might be relevant could include:

- Kelly's theatrical context, affecting the style, structure, characterization and themes

- the 21st century setting, affecting language and theme

- scientific advances in DNA, relating to plot and theme

- the profiling of school bullies, relating to character and theme

- the religious context, relating to Adam's role as well as to the fates of those involved in his death

- the geographical context, defining the plot and action.

Phil

Phil is the play's frequently silent **protagonist** who saves the group from the consequences of their attack on Adam, but at a cost to his own well-being. He starts the play as the unresponsive 'boyfriend' of Leah, whom he refuses to speak to.

He doesn't speak, either, when Jan and Mark arrive, but he obeys their summons, suggesting that he recognizes John Tate's authority. He listens, in silence, to Jan and Mark's account of the events that have led to Adam's 'death' but instantly assumes control when John Tate appeals to his 'cleverness'.

Phil's meticulous and complex plan reveals that he knows the strengths and weaknesses of the other group members as well as revealing an active and highly intelligent brain behind his silent façade. This key quotation is the first of many occasions when he recommends silence as a tactical device.

> **Key quotation**
>
> if everyone keeps their mouths shut we should be fine
>
> *(Phil, One, A Wood)*

Phil does not speak again until he needs to persuade an agitated Brian to go back to the police station and falsely identify the postman as Adam's abductor. Here, we see two new aspects of Phil's character. He can pretend to have a 'warm' and friendly side as he *'walks over to BRIAN and lays a hand on his shoulder'* (Two, A Wood). He speaks to Brian confidentially and in a 'man-to-man' style at first. When this doesn't have the effect he intended, we see a truly heartless and sadistic side to Phil.

> **Key quotation**
>
> Yes, yes, shhhh, yes. Sorry. You have to go in. Or we'll take you up the grille.
>
> *Pause.*
>
> We'll throw you in.
>
> *(Phil, Two, A Wood)*

Once Brian has agreed to go back, Phil repeats his instruction to the group to **'Keep your mouths shut'** before casually starting to *'eat his pie'* (Two, A Wood).

Phil uses his kindly façade again when he encourages the disorientated Adam to go back to his hedge and then reassures Lou that all will be well.

Key quotations

PHIL: Do you want to stay?

Pause. ADAM thinks. Looks at PHIL.

PHIL smiles, kindly. Nods.

(Three, A Wood)

LOU: What about… What about Cathy?

PHIL goes to her. Places a hand on her shoulder, smiles, warm, reassuring.

PHIL: Everything is going to be fine.

(Three, A Wood)

Phil's ability to switch **personas** instantly from cool and silent to warm and reassuring could be interpreted as a hallmark of a psychopathic personality, one that disregards normal social and moral responsibilities as well as the feelings and safety of others.

persona the part that a character or the narrator adopts in a literary work

protagonist the main character in a work of drama or fiction

Activity 1

Make a list of the things that Phil does, or doesn't do, that suggest he may have a psychopathic personality.

Phil's other prominent characteristic is his dependence on junk food. In almost every scene, he is either eating or drinking. He consumes ice cream, sweets, crisps, Coke, cakes and pastries, all of which are full of 'empty' calories, giving quick bursts of energy but no health benefits. In Two, he merely picks his teeth, presumably after having eaten something.

Only in the final scene, with Leah gone and knowing that he is responsible for a cold-blooded murder, we read: *'PHIL is not eating. He stares into the distance'* (Four, A Field). Kelly uses this change in Phil's behaviour to signal to the audience that he has experienced a massive and catastrophic shift in his relationship with the world. Now, without both Leah and his snacks, he seems a broken figure.

Activity 2

What effects do you think Phil's constant consumption of junk food has? Do you think Kelly might be linking sugar and salt to Phil's disturbed personality? Or does Phil simply eat to avoid talking to Leah? Draw up a table of what Phil eats, noting when and how it might link to his state of mind.

Tips for assessment

Because the characters in *DNA* are quite sketchily drawn, make sure that when answering a question about character you include details of what distinguishes one character from another. For example, only Phil is shown eating and drinking.

Phil's intelligence is largely criminal, rather than intellectual or emotional. He doesn't engage with Leah as she explores the natural world or raises ideas about fatalism and free will. He doesn't respond to her emotionally when she looks to him for reassurance or comfort. Phil only speaks Leah's name when they are alone together, to try to call her back when she finally deserts him.

Phil's criminal intelligence, however, is highly developed. While Leah's curiosity about the natural world and its significance is arguably stimulated by news stories, TV documentaries and reading non-fiction, the 'knowledge' that Phil displays seems to come directly from TV detective series.

At the end of the play, Phil appears withdrawn, dazed and completely unresponsive. He has lost Leah and isolated himself from the group, showing no interest in Richard's news about them. Phil's staring *'into the distance'* and *'staring at nothing'* are troubling symptoms of mental anguish or depression *(Four, A Field)*.

Like the other group members, Phil's life has been changed forever by the 'Adam' incident.

Activity 3

Leah sometimes asks Phil, **'What are you thinking?'** because she finds him so mysterious and puzzling *(One, A Field 1)*. Go back through the final scene between Phil and Richard, and write out what you think Phil's thoughts are as Richard talks and talks.

Phil is associated with themes of leadership, loyalty, speech and silence, truth and lies.

Leah

Leah is the most developed of all the characters in *DNA*. She is intelligent, curious and self-critical. Her main fault is her unswerving loyalty to Phil. From her first appearance, Kelly shows us how Leah defines herself in terms of Phil's opinion of her: **'I mean is it a negative, are you thinking a negative thing about –'** *(One, A Field 1)*.

Although Leah does not always express herself clearly or succinctly, she has a lot to say and what she says is almost always thoughtful and thought provoking. Leah admits to Phil that, **'I talk too much'** *(One, A Field 1)*, but she is the only character in the play to talk about matters beyond the immediate concerns of the group and the only one to reflect seriously on the consequences of what happened to Adam and on what that has done to the group.

Leah is intelligent enough to understand the implications of Phil's original solution to the 'death' of Adam, but she admires Phil too much to object. For the same reason, she doesn't interfere when Phil threatens to kill Brian even though she accepts that Phil is 'always serious' about what he says *(Two, A Wood)*. His plan to abandon the mentally fragile Adam in 'his hedge' *(Three, A Wood)*, however, is a step too far for Leah and she does try to intervene.

Key quotation

We can't leave him here, I mean that's not, are you serious? Are you seriously –

Alright, yes, there'll be –

Phil, this is insane. I mean I've never, but this, because, alright, whatever, but this is actually insane. We can't just leave him up here.

(Leah, Three, A Wood)

Leah knows that what has happened to Adam is terrible and that the cover-up is wrong. Sometimes she seems overwhelmed and appears to want to go outside the group to try to explain the situation to 'them' – the adults or the authorities.

In scenes where Leah and Phil are alone, she acts as a 'conscience' figure for Phil, but he ignores all her promptings of conscience and concentrates instead on his food.

Key quotations

We're in trouble now, Phil. Don't know how this'll pan out.

(Leah, One, A Field 2)

What have we done, Phil?

(Leah, Two, A Field 1)

Because this is a bit… isn't it. I mean this is really, talk about a bolt from the, yeah, shit. No, not shit, I mean it's good […] it's, it's good, Adam, that found, but I mean yes, it does make things a bit

(Leah, Three, A Wood)

Let's, come on, let's, it won't be that bad, it'll be, we can explain, we can talk. We can go through the whole thing and make them understand –

(Leah, Three, A Wood)

No! Stop, don't, don't, Phil, don't, what are you doing, what are you…

(Leah, Three, A Wood)

Leah did nothing to hurt Adam, yet she accepts joint responsibility for his 'death'. Nor does she try to excuse herself from the consequences of the callous or foolish actions of the others.

The audience is shocked when Leah produces the remains of Jerry in her Tupperware box because she has appeared to be the most moral of all the characters. Perhaps Kelly is suggesting that she had to do something to be ashamed of in order to empathize with the rest of the group.

Leah's relationship with Phil forms the core of the sub-plot. Like her, the audience anticipates a moment when he will reply to her. None of her strategies for attracting his attention succeed, however. Only her silence reaches him.

Leah and Phil on the field set for the National Theatre production at the Cottesloe Theatre, 2008

Leah experiences her own revelation about Phil when he ignores her pleas to save Adam. She finally rejects him when she spits out the only sweet we see him share with her.

> **Key quotation**
>
> **PHIL: He's dead. Everyone thinks he's dead. What difference will it make?**
>
> *She stares at him.*
>
> **LEAH: But he's not dead. He's alive.**
>
> *(Three, A Wood)*

> **Activity 4**
>
> Leah's silence and absence seem to affect Phil more profoundly than her chatter and presence ever did. Why do you think this is? Write the possible reasons for this as a series of bullet points.

Leah is associated with themes of loyalty, responsibility, the wider universe, cruelty and self-sacrifice.

John Tate

John Tate is the only character in the play with a surname. This may be to distinguish him as the leader of the group. A full name is more formal and less friendly than simply 'John', possibly suggesting that his name is notorious in school because of his reputation for being 'hard'.

John Tate takes the credit for the group's new status in the school and uses this to bolster his position as leader.

> **Key quotation**
>
> you can walk down any corridor in this [...] school and you know, no one bothers you and if you want something it's yours and no one bothers you and everyone respects you and everyone's scared of you and who made that, I mean I'm not boasting, but who made that happen?
>
> *(John Tate, One, A Wood)*

Tate's leadership is tested by the 'death' of Adam and he confesses to finding the situation, **'all quite stressful'** *(One, A Wood),* a dangerous admission for a leader.

He does not join in Jan and Mark's description of the torture of Adam, although they implicate him in it by repeating the phrase **'eh John'** in their story *(One, A Wood).* After listening to the re-telling of what the group has inflicted upon the boy, Tate seems to realize that this is one situation he can't get them out of. Certainly, it brings him to break his own ban on the word 'dead' and to admit, **'Dead. He's dead'** *(One, A Wood),* before turning to Phil and Leah, and effectively resigning control of the group.

> **Key quotation**
>
> Cathy says you're clever.
>
> So. What do we do?
>
> *(John Tate, One, A Wood)*

John Tate does not speak again in the play. He fulfils the role Phil assigns him in the cover-up, which involves perverting the course of justice by making a false witness statement to the police. Later, he is reported by Leah to have **'lost it'** and **'won't come out of his room'** *(Two, A Field 1).* This may be as a result of his part in Adam's 'death', of his involvement in deceiving the police, of having yielded his leadership to Phil, or a combination of all these things.

Eventually, Richard tells Phil that **'John Tate's found god'** and that he's **'joined the Jesus Army'** *(Four, A Field).* Guilt has caused Tate to seek strength outside himself and to look for membership of a different type of group – one based on a philosophy of goodness and love.

John Tate is associated with themes of leadership, power and violence (bullying), good and evil, loyalty, truth and lies, as well as guilt and religion.

His function is to act as an example of one type of leadership and, through his later finding of God, to demonstrate the transformative effect of Adam's death on his 'watch'.

> **Activity 5**
>
> Why do you think John Tate hands over leadership of the group to Phil and then joins the **'Jesus Army'**? Prepare a presentation to explain your ideas.

Richard

We hear about Richard before we meet him, when Lou identifies him as the one person, other than John Tate, that she is 'scared of' in school *(One, A Wood)*. When John Tate tells Richard, 'I'm gonna hurt you, actually', if he uses the word 'dead' again, Richard responds in a mature and measured way, telling him directly, 'You shouldn't threaten me, John' *(One, A Wood)*.

Kelly is able to suggest a previous power struggle between John Tate and Richard very economically, through John Tate's reaction to the idea that Richard has turned against him.

> **Key quotation**
>
> Because if you've got a side that means you're not on my side and if you're not on my side that means you're setting yourself up against me and I thought we'd got over all that silliness.
>
> *(John Tate, One, A Wood)*

Richard's reassurance that 'we are mates now' brings calm to the situation *(One, A Wood)*.

Although not leader material himself, Richard is the one Phil chooses to take Brian to the Head to report the sighting of the man in the woods, suggesting that Phil sees him as someone the teachers will trust. Richard is 'open mouthed' and in complete awe of Phil, once the other boy has finished outlining his clever scheme *(One, A Wood)*.

> **Activity 6**
>
> Where would you place Richard in the group hierarchy? Draw a chart to show your understanding of the relative status of group members.

In Two, Richard is stunned by Cathy's stupidity in deliberately incriminating the postman over Adam's disappearance: 'What we wanted was to cover up what had happened, not to frame someone else' *(Two, A Wood)*. He also blames Mark, who was Cathy's partner in Phil's scheme, greeting him with, 'You dick, Mark', when he arrives with Brian *(Two, A Wood)*.

However, when Phil threatens to kill Brian, Richard's objection is a weak, 'Er, Phil', and he seems powerless to deter him *(Two, A Wood)*.

Richard is not present when Adam resurfaces and, presumably, he never learns about his execution. The only news of Richard, before his final appearance, is what Leah tells Phil – 'Richard's named his dog Adam' *(Three, A Field 1)* – which suggests that he has a troubled conscience.

In the final scene of the play, Richard appears in the field with Phil and acts as a substitute for Leah. Like Leah, he tries and fails to attract Phil's attention. Richard does handstands that Phil *'doesn't even look at'* *(Four, A Field)*. He pleads with Phil to return to the group.

> **Key quotation**
>
> Everyone's asking after you. [...] What do you think about that?
>
> *(Richard, Four, A Field)*

Eventually, Richard talks about himself and reveals that he has just had an 'unreal' experience as he came up to the field, when he was enveloped in a cloud of **'fluff, like dandelions'** *(Four, A Field)*, which provoked a revelation about the universe. This is similar to Leah's experience of déjà vu at the end of Two, representing, for each of the characters, a moment of certainty in an uncertain world.

> **Key quotation**
>
> And in that second, Phil, I knew that there was life on other planets. I knew we weren't alone in the universe, I didn't just think it or feel it, I knew it
>
> *(Richard, Four, A Field)*

Phil continues to be unresponsive and the scene and the play end with him and Richard sitting *'in silence' (Four, A Field)*.

Richard is associated with themes of leadership, right and wrong, conscience and intelligence.

His function is to replace Leah in the field scene and reveal Phil's descent into apathy (a total lack of interest).

Activity 7

What are Richard's feelings for Phil, in your opinion? What kind of relationship does Richard have with each of the other group members? Describe Richard's relationship with each character, writing one sentence for each, supported with a quotation from the text.

Tips for assessment

Sometimes the absence of a character in a particular scene is significant. For example, neither Richard nor Danny is on stage when Adam comes back 'from the dead'. You must be able to show that you understand the implications of one character or another not being aware of the 'total picture'.

Cathy

Cathy is a dangerous character. While Brian arrives in the group hideout in the wood *'crying'* because of what has happened to Adam, Cathy is *'grinning'* *(One, A Wood)*. She seems to enjoy the excitement of Adam's 'death' and describes the situation as *'mad'* but *'quite exciting as well'* *(One, A Wood)*. Not only does she show no remorse, she shows a real enjoyment in the incident.

> **Key quotation**
>
> Better than ordinary life. *(Cathy, One, A Wood)*

Cathy tries to cause trouble for both Danny and Richard by suggesting to John Tate that they are on a different 'side' from John and she almost succeeds in creating a rift between the boys. She and Danny don't like one another, perhaps because Danny is intelligent and possibly studious, as he plans to be a dentist, while Cathy is evidently unintelligent and lives for thrills. It is she who has described Phil and Leah as *'clever'* to John Tate *(One, A Wood)*, which could also suggest that she feels inferior to the more intelligent members of the group.

Cathy accepts her assigned role in the cover-up (breaking into Adam's house and collecting DNA of a random stranger) without hesitation, only asking questions to clarify instructions.

After the postman has been arrested, Cathy is exhilarated and flattered that the reporters wanted to interview her. She is oblivious to the potential injustice of framing an innocent man and thinks only of herself and how she might benefit from events. Her excitement is somewhat crushed when the others turn on her for using her *'initiative'* and she does not speak again in the scene *(Two, A Wood)*.

> **Key quotation**
>
> Well, we thought, you know, I mean you'd given a description so we thought, well, I thought, you know, show initiative, we'll look for a fat balding postman with bad teeth.
>
> *They stare at her.*
>
> *(Cathy, Two, A Wood)*

However, the next time we hear of her, Cathy has recovered her self-importance, appeared *'on the telly'* and been treated like a *'celebrity'* in school *(Three, A Field 1)*. In Three, Brian explains how Cathy *'loves violence now'*, a fact she does not deny *(Three, A Wood)*.

> **Key quotation**
>
> I threatened to gouge one of his eyes out. *(Cathy, Three, A Wood)*

Cathy also slaps Brian in an unprovoked attack and threatens him with 'If you don't shut up you'll be dead' *(Three, A Wood)*.

Phil finds it easy to use Cathy's new love of violence to manipulate her into killing Adam. She has already demonstrated a complete lack of conscience as well as an inability to distinguish or abide by moral boundaries. This is confirmed by Richard when he updates Phil about the rest of the group at the end of the play.

> **Key quotation**
>
> Cathy doesn't care. She's too busy running things. You wouldn't believe how things have got, Phil. She's insane. She cut a first year's finger off, that's what they say anyway.
>
> *(Richard, Four, A Field)*

Cathy has progressed from being a rather unintelligent group member, willing to obey others, to terrorizing the first year, with Lou as her 'sidekick'. Unlike the other group members, she has developed a real taste for power and the violence required to maintain it, and she is on the road to a lifetime of deviant or criminal behaviour.

Cathy is associated with the themes of good and evil, right and wrong, violence, bullying and intelligence.

Her function is to demonstrate how violence has the power to corrupt.

> **Activity 8**
>
> Do you think that Kelly portrays Cathy in a wholly negative way or does she have any positive characteristics? Draw two columns and make a list of all Cathy's negative qualities on one side, then see if you can find some positive features for the second column.

Danny

Danny is a boy with ambitions to be a dentist and these ambitions define the way he reacts to events. Although he is a part of the group that bullied Adam, he clearly has not thought about the consequences of his actions and he seems to see Adam's 'death' as an inconvenience that threatens his plans.

> **Key quotation**
>
> This is not part of the plan. Dental college is part of the plan, A-levels are part of the plan, dead people are not part of the plan, this is not Dental college.
>
> *(Danny, One, A Wood)*

Danny reveals himself to be a self-centered and somewhat insensitive character, who shows no remorse for what he has been a part of. He stands up to John Tate, briefly, when he tries to ban the word 'dead'. However, once friction erupts between Richard and John Tate, his instinct for self-preservation ensures that he will not 'side' with the less powerful Richard and he completely accepts John Tate's inadequate 'solution' to the 'Adam' issue.

> **Key quotation**
>
> I want to keep calm, I want to say nothing, just like you, you're right, you're right, John.
>
> *(Danny, One, A Wood)*

There is tension between Danny and Cathy, as Leah reminds Phil in Two: 'Remember last month, Dan threatened to kill Cathy?' *(Two, A Field 1)*. In One, Danny twice tells Cathy to 'shut up': once when she expresses excitement about what has happened to Adam and again when she tells Danny to shut up when he is defending Richard.

Interestingly, when Phil assigns roles to the group to help to cover up what has really happened to Adam, he groups Danny with Cathy and Mark to break into Adam's house. Only Danny protests at this, understandably fearful of being implicated further.

Later in the play, when the innocent postman has been arrested, Danny is shocked by the turn of events. However, his main concern is for himself and his career: 'This sort of stuff sticks, you know' *(Two, A Wood)*.

> **Key quotation**
>
> You need three references for dental college, how am I gonna get references?
>
> *(Danny, Two, A Wood)*

Danny is brighter than Lou and Cathy, so the full implications of Cathy's use of her 'initiative' to target an actual postal worker to frame for Adam's abduction strike him immediately and his reactions are intense: 'Oh my god', 'Oh, Jesus' *(Two, A Wood)*.

> **Key quotation**
>
> We can't let them think it's him. I mean, I really can't be mixed up in something like that, it wouldn't be right.
>
> *(Danny, Two, A Wood)*

When Brian refuses to go back to the police to identify the postman, Danny sees no alternative, insisting, 'We can't do nothing, they want Brian' *(Two, A Wood)*. He is stunned when Phil tells Brian 'we'll take you up the grille. *Pause.* We'll throw you in'. Genuinely shocked, Danny asks, 'Is he serious?' Once Phil has persuaded Brian to 'help us', Danny and the others 'stare at' Phil, but nobody intervenes *(Two, A Wood)*. The future dentist Danny simply accepts the course of action Phil proposes.

Danny does not appear in the play again. It may be assumed that he has attempted to distance himself from the rest of the group because he does not want to jeopardize his future.

While Danny's self-interest is an unattractive quality, Kelly's presentation of the character provides some light relief within the play. His obsession with teeth, for example, creates humour even in the darkest moments.

Danny is associated with themes of ambition, right and wrong, truth and lies, loyalty and self-preservation.

His function is to highlight the varied make-up of the group and to add some humour to the play.

Activity 9

How does a 'nice' boy like Danny get involved in the bullying of Adam? Write two paragraphs to summarize your thoughts about this. Remember to support your work with close reference to the play text.

Tips for assessment

Despite the play's serious message about the consequences of bullying, Kelly's **tone** is sometimes humorous. Make sure that you mention this if you are considering Kelly's creation of mood or atmosphere, especially if you are exploring an extract from the play.

tone mood or attitude

Brian

If John Tate is at the top of the hierarchy within the original group, Brian is at the bottom. Richard openly admits to hating Brian, Phil threatens to kill him when he refuses to identify the postman and Cathy slaps him, to get him to **'shut up'** *(Three, A Wood)*. Nobody objects to this mistreatment of him.

John Tate and Brian, the top and bottom of the original hierarchy

Brian's motive for hanging around with the others and for being involved in Adam's persecution may be to deflect their negative attention from himself on to someone even weaker.

For most of his early appearances, Brian is described as *'crying'*; he appears weak. Yet he is the only character with the moral fibre to oppose John Tate's original decision that the group should stay calm and **'say nothing'** about Adam's 'death' *(One, A Wood)*. Until threatened by Phil with a similar fate to Adam's, Brian appears to have the most developed conscience about what the group has done, and he puts forward the suggestion that they **'should tell someone'** *(One, A Wood)*.

Phil exploits Brian's capacity for crying, choosing him to be the one to report to the Head that a man showed him **'his willy in the woods'** *(One, A Wood)*. Brian barely protests at first, merely uttering a confused, **'Wha… what?'**, but his conscience won't allow him to implicate an innocent man. Once the suspect has been arrested, Brian is described by Danny as **'Hiding'** and by Lou as **'shitting it'** *(Two, A Wood)*, while Brian himself stresses that he won't return to the police station.

> **Key quotation**
>
> I can't face it. They look at me. They look at me like I'm lying and it makes me cry. I can't stand the way they look at me. And then, because I cry, they think I'm telling the truth, but I'm crying because I'm lying and I feel terrible inside.
>
> *(Brian, Two, A Wood)*

The sincerity of Brian's distress seems to touch both Lou and Leah, but Phil is less sympathetic. When Brian resists Phil's attempt to coax him into doing what he wants, Phil threatens him with the same 'death' that Adam suffered. Faced with such a choice, Brian agrees to lie again but his second, more serious involvement in the cover-up costs him his sanity.

> **Key quotation**
>
> Brian's on medication. Did you know that? Phil? Did you know that they've put Brian on medication? […] Yep, Brian's off his head
>
> *(Leah, Three, A Field 1)*

The next time we see Brian, the combination of his medication (presumably for depression) and his happiness at discovering Adam causes him to appear slightly mad. He eats earth, talks about the trees **'watching'** him and the day **'licking our skin'** *(Three, A Wood)*. Cathy slaps Brian suddenly and he simply breaks into giggles. Brian is the only character who is entirely positive about Adam's 'return' and this may be attributed as much to his medication as to his kindly nature.

Kelly uses Brian's very evident mental breakdown as a physical representation of the workings of guilt and a bad conscience on a basically moral person. The very strong visual image of Phil's 'experiment' with a zombie-like Brian, as he places the plastic bag over his head, is one of the most shocking moments of the play.

Phil continues to exploit Brian's vulnerability when he instructs him to take Adam back to the hedge and then sends him with Cathy to assist in the cold-blooded murder of Adam. Although Brian seems incapable of understanding the reality of the situation, pitifully exclaiming, **'This is brilliant'** *(Three, A Wood)*, his involvement in Adam's death and the framing of an innocent man leads him to complete mental collapse and the possibility of going into a mental institution.

> **Key quotation**
>
> **Brian's on stronger and stronger medication. They caught him staring at a wall and drooling last week. It's either drooling or giggling. Keeps talking about earth. I think they're going to section him.**
>
> *(Richard, Four, A Field)*

Brian is associated with the themes of bullying, good and evil, truth and lies, empathy and conscience.

His function is to represent a weakling figure in the hierarchy.

Activity 10

Brian does not seem to fit in with the group at all. Why do you think the rest of the group let him be a part of the group that get to **'come here in the woods'** *(One, A Wood)*? Write your ideas in bullet points.

Mark and Jan

Mark and Jan always appear together and do not have many distinguishing characteristics. In the first scene, although Jan is shocked to hear about Adam's death and Mark is also adamant that **'it's not funny'** *(One, A Street)*, neither focus on the human tragedy that they have been part of or appear to feel guilty or remorseful.

Both are nasty bullies whose description of how Adam was tortured, and then stoned to his death, form a horrific part of the narrative. When explaining Adam's 'last' hours to Phil and Leah, Jan and Mark launch into a lively and sickening joint description of what the group did to Adam. Neither of them names who did what. It is left to Mark to describe Adam's final moments since Jan has gone home. Mark refers vaguely to **'someone'** having **'pegged'** (thrown) a stone at Adam, making everyone laugh and causing the group to join in.

> **Key quotation**
>
> **So we're all peggin them. Laughing. And his face, it's just making you laugh harder and harder, and they're getting nearer and nearer. And one hits his head. And the shock on his face is so... funny. And we're all just...**
>
> **just...**
>
> **really chucking these stones into him, really hard and laughing and he slips.**
>
> *(Mark, One, A Wood)*

Both Jan and Mark refer to Adam's 'fear' and to the fact that he was 'scared' and 'terrified', and yet both insist that Adam was 'having a laugh' with them and that they were all 'in stitches'. Both appear to believe that it was a teenage escapade that somehow went 'a bit far' *(One, A Wood)*.

Mark and Jan are sucked into Phil's strategy to avoid detection and neither raises the slightest objection either to breaking into Adam's house (Mark) or to riding on Danny's back in the wood to create the impression of the weight of the 'fat postman' (Jan) *(One, A Wood)*.

Later, we hear that Mark has told Brian that he's 'gotta go' to the police to identify the suspect *(Two, A Street)* and Jan agrees. Mark's inability to prevent Cathy from framing an innocent man suggests that he is weak and his somewhat lame excuse, 'It was her idea' *(Two, A Wood)*, shows him to be a disloyal, as well as an ineffectual, character.

Both Mark and Jan are changed by their involvement in Adam's 'death'. Mark takes up 'charity work' and Jan is in 'Floods of tears' at Adam's memorial service *(Three, A Field 1)*. Jan is also seen 'helping a first year find the gym' *(Three, A Field 1)*, an action that is clearly out of character in Leah's opinion. These new activities suggest that the pair are feeling guilty about their behaviour and attempting to do some sort of **penance**.

> **penance** (in the Christian church) an act or deed done to make amends for a 'sin' committed

Jan and Mark are presented as never knowing what to do. After Adam's reappearance, they remain incapable of thinking strategically, each asking desperately, 'What are we going to do?' *(Three, A Wood)*. They gladly accept Phil's instruction to leave, although Jan seeks reassurance, asking him, 'Are we going to be in trouble' *(Three, A Wood)*.

Key quotation

PHIL: If you go now and you say nothing to no one about this, you won't be in trouble.

She thinks. Nods to MARK. They go.

(Three, A Wood)

The fact that Jan 'thinks' suggests that she has at least an inkling that Phil is going to 'solve' the problem of Adam 'once and for all', and both she and Mark, by leaving, are partly complicit in Adam's 'second' death.

It is unsurprising to the audience when we hear that Mark and Jan have become shoplifters, since they have shown a distinct lack of moral direction from the beginning. Kelly suggests that they will join the criminal class when they leave school rather than becoming law-abiding members of society.

Jan and Mark are associated with themes of violence and bullying, right and wrong, crime and initiative.

Their function is to act as a Chorus for the audience and create anticipation and tension in the street scenes.

Activity 11

Of all of the characters responsible for bullying Adam, only Jan and Mark speak about their involvement in the incident. Write a paragraph explaining why you think Kelly focuses on Jan and Mark's experience of the events and does not include anyone else's.

Lou

Lou is the least memorable and least developed character. She demonstrates a pessimistic outlook on life, always fearing the worst in any situation. She is blunt in her dealings with fellow group members but is not very bright and is definitely a follower rather than a leader.

Lou's motivation, throughout, is to save her own skin and by the end of the play she has transferred her loyalty to Cathy. Richard tells Phil that Lou has become Cathy's 'best friend', summing this up as a 'Dangerous game' *(Four, A Field)*.

Although part of the initial bullying and complicit in Phil's cover-up plan, Lou takes no part in the final killing of Adam. However, by obeying Phil's order to go home and not to speak about Adam's reappearance to anyone, she follows her instinct for self-preservation.

Lou is associated with themes of bullying, hierarchy within the group, and good and evil.

Her function is to demonstrate the effect of criminality on a weak character.

Activity 12

Imagine that you have been asked to choose the actress to play Lou. Based on what you understand of her character, what characteristics do you think would be appropriate? Think about her physical appearance and her voice as well as the ways she stands and moves. Justify your decisions from the text.

Adam

Adam's name does not appear in the cast list, either in the printed text or in theatre programmes. Instead, he is referred to simply as 'Boy', as Kelly no doubt wanted to surprise the audience with Adam's survival.

On stage, he appears to be seriously disturbed and we don't learn much about his character from his garbled account of himself. Instead, we rely mainly on the other characters' descriptions of him to understand his character.

> **Key quotation**
>
> You know Adam, you know what he's like, so we were sort of, well, alright, taking the piss, sort of. You know what he's like he was, sort of hanging around
>
> *(Mark, One, A Wood)*

We know from Leah that Adam has invited members of the group to his birthday parties in the past and that they have attended them, despite taking 'the piss' about the cheapness of the ice cream on offer *(Three, A Wood)*. This shows that Adam counted them as friends at one time.

Although it is not stated explicitly, it is implied that when Adam ate leaves, burned his socks, stole alcohol and ran across a motorway, he believed that these acts were part of some initiation ceremony that would prove him to be worthy to join John Tate's exclusive group. As Mark describes it, the group were trying to see 'how far he'll go' *(One, A Wood)*, and Adam was certainly prepared to go a long way to be accepted as a member. Such membership, as John Tate boasts, ensures that 'no-one bothers you and everyone respects you and everyone's scared of you' *(One, A Wood)*. To a boy who has suffered at the hands of ruthless bullies, these long-term benefits may have seemed worth a little short-term pain and humiliation. Instead, drunk on stolen vodka and emboldened by their herd mentality, the group – though evidently surprised and even impressed by Adam's daring in 'walking on the grille' – begins to stone him 'just for the laugh' *(One, A Wood)*.

When Adam appears in Three, the audience see a boy who has been living off vegetation and insects since his ordeal and sleeping rough in a hideout made of cardboard and rags inside a hedge. Adam is completely disorientated and, beyond knowing his own name, he claims to have no recollection of what happened to him.

> **Key quotation**
>
> *They stand around a boy who looks like a tramp. His clothes are torn and dirty and his hair is matted with dried blood from an old gash on his forehead that has not been cleaned up.*
>
> *(Three, A Wood)*

Adam reappears, looking 'like a tramp' and covered in dried blood

Kelly presents Adam's experience of waking and crawling out of a series of tunnels into the light as an 'out-of-body' experience, similar to a 'rebirth'.

Key quotation

Came outside.

I couldn't remember things.

I couldn't remember anything.

I was new.

A new

a new

a new me. And I felt

happy.

(Adam, Three, A Wood)

There are some interesting possibilities about Kelly's decision to name his victim figure Adam since, in the Bible, Adam was the name of the first man that God created. In the Bible story, Adam and Eve disobeyed God's instruction not to eat the apple from the Tree of Knowledge. As a punishment, they were expelled from the Garden of Eden into the wilderness. This event is referred to as 'the fall' of man. It is possible that Adam's literal fall is **symbolic**, since he does not return to his home, living instead in his man-made wilderness in the hedge.

However, this is not the only possible **allegorical** interpretation of Adam. Some commentators have compared Adam to a Christ-like figure, who is sacrificed for the good of the group. According to the Bible, Jesus Christ was the son of God, who sacrificed him to redeem humanity. He died a horrific death by crucifixion after having been tormented and physically abused. He had nails driven into the palms of his hands and the soles of his feet, he was made to wear a crown of thorns and he was taunted as he died upon the cross. After three days, he rose from the dead and was seen by some of his followers. Adam in the play also appears to rise from the dead, emerging from the tunnel. Adam himself says, 'I thought I was dead' and, after being 'reborn', he is discovered by Brian and Cathy 'up the hill' *(Three, A Wood)*.

Key quotation

What's more important; one person or everyone?

(Phil, Three, A Field)

---

allegorical having a spiritual, moral or political meaning clearly symbolic of something else

symbolic acting as a symbol; something that represents ideas beyond itself, e.g. Adam's fall through the grille might represent Adam and Eve's expulsion from the Garden of Eden

Activity 13

Re-read Mark and Jan's description of the bullying of Adam just before his fall into the grille. Make a list of the similarities that you can see between what the bullies did to him and what Jesus suffered before his crucifixion.

> **Key quotations**
>
> John Tate's found God [...] He's joined the Jesus Army *(Four, A Field)*
>
> Mark's been doing charity work *(Three, A Field 1)*
>
> Richard's named his dog Adam *(Three, A Field 1)*
>
> Mark's mum says if her baby's a boy she's going to call him Adam *(Three, A Field 1)*
>
> They're naming the science lab after him *(Three, A Wood)*
>
> Suddenly Adam's everyone's best friend *(Three, A Field 1)*
>
> Funny thing is they're all actually behaving better as well *(Three, A Field 1)*
>
> Everyone's happier. It's pouring into the school, grief, grief is making them happy. *(Two, A Field 1)*

Adam's ordeal has apparently transformed him as well as other characters. His explanation of how he emerged from the tunnel is both disturbing and moving for the audience, which has had the image of his suffering in mind since Mark described it earlier in the play.

> **Key quotation**
>
> And I do know my name so you can shut, you can…
>
> I live there. It's
>
> mine, I
>
> live
>
> there.
>
> Adam.
>
> I'm not coming back.
>
> *Beat.*
>
> It's Adam.
>
> *(Adam, Three, A Wood)*

Adam's reappearance is only welcomed by Brian, in his befuddled state. For the others, Adam's survival, though miraculous, is no cause for celebration. When Phil asks Adam, **'Do you want to come back?'** *(Three, A Wood)*, Adam's reply is ambiguous. First he asks, **'What?'**, then he starts, but does not complete his sentence, saying only **'I'**. Phil speaks kindly to him, **'Do you want to stay?'**. Kelly's stage direction is simply, *'Pause. ADAM thinks. Looks at PHIL'* *(Three, A Wood)*, and Adam then allows himself to be led back to his hedge by Brian.

This is the last we see of Adam, a bewildered, bloodstained boy, being led offstage by an equally bewildered boy, who will later assist in the murder of this 'Mate' that only he is pleased to see alive. It is a very powerful moment on stage.

Adam is linked with themes of bullying, belonging, faith, religion, sacrifice, violence and friendship.

His function is to symbolize the victim figure in the group and to embody the notion of sacrifice.

Activity 14

'ADAM thinks' is a very unusual stage direction *(Three, A Wood)*. How might an actor perform the act of thinking, at this point in the play? Write down what you believe Adam is thinking at this point.

The adult world

No adults appear on stage, but the teenagers do refer to adult figures from time to time, although they choose not to engage with authority figures, their parents, teachers or the police, when they find themselves in trouble.

The adults who are mentioned, in passing, include:

- The school head teacher
- Mark's mother, who is expecting a baby
- Adam's parents, who appear on TV, appealing to the abductor to return Adam
- the postman Cathy frames for the abduction
- the police, who are questioning the suspect and looking for Brian
- some reporters, who tell Richard and Cathy about the DNA evidence
- the dentist where Danny does his work experience.

None of these figures play any part in the play other than helping to establish a world beyond the street, the field and the wood where the story unfolds.

Tips for assessment

It's important to note the absence of adults and the significance of their absence.

catalyst something that brings about a change of direction in the story

foil a character that contrasts with another in order to show up certain qualities or failings

Writing about characters

You may be asked to write about one or more characters and to consider either how Kelly presents each character or how he uses individual characters to communicate his ideas.

Always try to refer to the following, where applicable:

- the appearance of the character if stated in the play
- what the character says about themselves and about others
- what other characters say about them
- comparisons and/or contrasts with other characters
- what the character does in the play, their actions and reactions to events
- the type of language they use.

When thinking about the purpose or function of the character, consider whether they:

- give information about offstage events or events that occurred before the play
- develop the plot
- act as a **foil** or contrast to other characters
- contribute to major themes of the play
- alter the mood or atmosphere, e.g. creating comedy or pathos
- act as a **catalyst**.

Character map

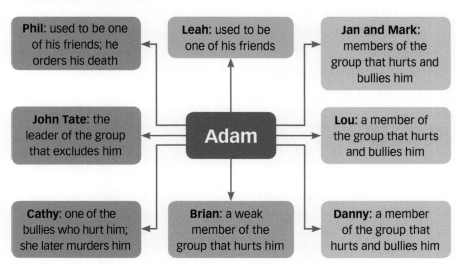

Phil: used to be one of his friends; he orders his death

Leah: used to be one of his friends

Jan and Mark: members of the group that hurts and bullies him

John Tate: the leader of the group that excludes him

Adam

Lou: a member of the group that hurts and bullies him

Cathy: one of the bullies who hurt him; she later murders him

Brian: a weak member of the group that hurts him

Danny: a member of the group that hurts and bullies him

Language

All plays are written to be performed on a stage in front of a live audience. In that situation, the language of the play is just one element (as well as, for example, movement, facial expression, set and costume) that affects the audience experience and understanding of the play. When we are studying a play rather than watching it, the language becomes the single most important way to understand the unfolding of the story, its main concerns and themes, and how to recognize the different characters.

In modern plays, we are aware of two different aspects of language in the text: the stage directions and the characters' dialogue.

Stage directions

The stage directions express the playwright's intentions for how the play is presented to an audience. They are written for the director of the play as well as for the actors. They may include:

- indications of where a scene is set, e.g. *DNA* begins with the direction, *'A Street. MARK and JAN' (One)*.
- indications of when the actors should *'Pause'* or where there should be *'Silence'* or *'More silence' (One, A Wood)*.
- sometimes, directions for how certain characters behave when they are not speaking, e.g. for how the characters react to Phil's strategy: *'They stare at him open mouthed' (One, A Wood)*.
- occasionally, how some of the individual lines should be delivered, e.g. when Leah tries to attract Phil's attention by strangling herself: *'(Gasping…) Phil! This is it…' (One, A Field 2)*.

In the direction below, Kelly wants Brian to behave in a specific way so gives him this clear direction. More frequently, Kelly leaves it to the dialogue itself to suggest the way that it is delivered.

> **Key quotation**
>
> *(Like it's hilarious.)* He's probably been eating earth!
>
> *(Brian, Three, A Wood)*

Activity 1

a) Choose any page from the section set in the wood in One. Add stage directions to each line to guide the actors in the way they should deliver their lines.

b) Write a paragraph, briefly summarizing what the exercise has taught you about Kelly's writing.

In the National Theatre production at the Cottesloe Theatre, 2008, the actors seem very isolated, which would set a particular tone for these scenes

Tips for assessment

Because stage directions are infrequent in *DNA*, it is important that you pay attention to them and refer to them in your assessment as this is Kelly's way of ensuring that his text is delivered exactly how he wants.

Dramatic language: characters' dialogue

Dramatic language usually consists of a combination of dialogue, **duologue** and monologue. Kelly uses all these forms of dramatic language in *DNA*.

duologue speech between two characters

The dramatic language of *DNA* is distinctive in that it is crafted to mimic everyday speech and to echo the way that modern teenagers communicate, informally, within their peer groups. Kelly also includes pauses, repetitions and hesitations within the speeches, some of which are made up of single words or phrases. Sometimes, speeches are incomplete and overlap with one another. At other times, there are deliberate interruptions. All are features of normal real-life conversations.

> **Key quotation**
>
> **DANNY:** He answers the description. Fat postman, thinning hair, his teeth are terrible, apparently.
>
> **LEAH:** But that's just
>
> **LOU:** Yeah. That's what we thought.
>
> **LEAH:** we just, didn't we, Phil, we just, we just, I mean you just…
>
> **DANNY:** What are we gonna do?
>
> **LOU:** We're screwed.
>
> **LEAH:** We're not…
>
> **LOU:** We're –
>
> **LEAH:** No, no, sorry, no we're not, are we Phil, I mean we're, no we're alright.
>
> *(Two, A Wood)*

In the key quotation above, you can see how many of Leah's lines are intended to be spoken continuously, when there are no full stops to signal a break in her speech. She uses very simple vocabulary as well as repetition to reveal the difficulty she is having in processing Danny's information: the 'filler' or 'empty' word 'just' is used four times in one brief, interrupted and incomplete sentence. She uses the negatives 'not' twice and 'no' four times within an utterance of only 17 words, showing how determined she is to reject Lou's opinion.

> **Activity 2**
>
> Find other examples from the play where characters cut off each other's speeches or where lines trail away. What precise effect do you think Kelly intends to create through these short and/or incomplete lines?

There are no adults in *DNA*, so the teenagers never have to speak formally or politely. Often, they are rude, hostile or belittling to one another. Some of the characters also swear.

Key quotations

Shut up, Danny.

(Cathy, One, A Wood)

That just leaves you, Brian. You crying little piece of filth.

(John Tate, One, A Wood)

You dick, Mark.

(Richard, Two, A Wood)

We're screwed.

(Lou, Two, A Wood)

Jesus Christ.

(Lou, Three, A Wood)

Activity 3

What do you think these accusations and expletives reveal about the speakers? For example does it suggest their sense of powerlessness or fear? Make a list of the various effects created when characters swear or abuse each other.

When John Tate tries to intimidate Danny or when Phil gives instructions, they speak authoritatively, their sentences are complete and they are not interrupted. In the first quotation below, John combines the insulting implication that Danny is being silly with the more menacing suggestion that this attitude is dangerous. In the second, Phil is not conversing with Richard, assuming the leadership of the group and telling him exactly what to do.

Key quotations

So if me and Richard are mates now, which we are and all that silliness is over, which it is, and you're on someone's side, Danny, then you're on your own side, which is very, well, to be honest, very silly and dangerous.

(John Tate, One, A Wood)

Richard, you take Brian to the Head, tell him that you found Brian crying in the toilets, asked him what was wrong and when he told you, you brought him here.

(Phil, One, A Wood)

Speech, fluency and social background

All the characters attend the same school. However, there are differences in the ways that they express themselves, indicating some distinctions in their levels of intelligence and/or in their social backgrounds.

Phil

The most articulate character is Phil. He uses Standard English and, when he does speak, he speaks in more or less complete sentences that are grammatically correct. Phil is authoritative, issues clear instructions and never swears.

Leah

Leah says the most in the play. When she is speaking to Phil, in the field, she often uses complete sentences and is capable of expressing complex thoughts.

Her speeches in the field could be described as being written in the style of **stream of consciousness**, reflecting the way her thoughts occur to her, develop and/or peter out. She uses the widest vocabulary of all the group, drawing on her interest in the world around her. She asks a lot of genuine questions as well as many **rhetorical questions**. Sometimes, her sentences trail away or are incomplete, even when she is speaking to Phil, especially when she is becoming frustrated with his silence.

> **Key quotation**
>
> People getting all upset about polluting the natural order? When this planet is churning molten lava with a thin layer of crust on top with a few kilometres of atmosphere clinging to it? I mean, please, don't gimme all that, carbon dioxide? Carbon dioxide, Phil? And look at the rest of the universe, Venus, Phil, there's a, look at Venus, what about Venus, hot enough to melt lead *(Leah, Two, A Field 1)*

In group situations, Leah's speech pattern is similar to the others', with half-finished sentences and incomplete **grammatical constructions**.

> **Key quotation**
>
> LOU: Good?
>
> LEAH: it's, yeah, yes it's
>
> JAN: How is it good?
>
> LEAH: it's, it's good, Adam, that found, but I mean yes, it does make things a bit
>
> LOU: Screwed?
>
> LEAH: tricky, no, not... don't say
>
> *(Three, A Wood)*

The first part of Leah's exchange with Lou in the key quotation opposite is expressed positively, even though ideas are incomplete: **'yeah'**, **'yes'**, **'it's good'**, **'yes'**. However, when Lou interrupts with the negative, **'Screwed?'**, Leah's words also become negative: **'no'**, **'not'**, **'don't'**. This shows that Leah is reacting quickly to Lou's challenge.

---

grammatical construction the way language is conventionally arranged into units to form sentences, made up of nouns, verbs, prepositions, conjunctions, adjectives and/or adverbs

rhetorical question a question that does not anticipate an answer but is used to create an effect

stream of consciousness a style of writing that mirrors a character's continuous and unedited thoughts

---

Activity 4

Write three paragraphs comparing Leah's use of language in different situations:

a) when she is alone with Phil in One

b) with John Tate in One

c) with Lou and Danny in the wood in Two.

Richard

Richard expresses himself clearly and forcefully, both in group scenes and in the final scene, when he tries to coax Phil back to the group. He is also capable of quite abstract thought and expression.

Richard seems more self-contained and sure of himself than most of the other characters, here in the Hull Truck Theatre Company production in 2012

> **Key quotation**
>
> I knew we weren't alone in the universe, I didn't just think it or feel it, I knew it, I know it, it was as if the universe was suddenly shifting and giving me a glimpse, this vision that could see everything, just for a fraction of a heartbeat of a second.
>
> (Richard, Four, A Field)

Danny

Danny wants to be a dentist and needs excellent qualifications to make the grade to join a university dental school. He uses Standard English, reflecting these ambitions, and tends to speak in complete, grammatically correct sentences.

> **Key quotation**
>
> We can't let them think it's him. I mean, I really can't be mixed up in something like that, it wouldn't be right.
>
> *(Danny, Two, A Wood)*

John Tate

John Tate, although a leader, is a more hesitant speaker than these others and struggles to find the right word, especially when he is under stress. This may suggest that, under pressure, his brain isn't functioning at normal speed.

> **Key quotation**
>
> JOHN TATE: It's a bit serious, but let's not, I mean come on, let's not over play the, the, the
>
> LOU: He's dead.
>
> JOHN TATE: the gravity of… Well, yes, okay, fair enough, but
>
> *(One, A Wood)*

Jan and Mark

Jan and Mark tend to speak in **monosyllables** and very brief sentences, except when they are narrating what the group did to Adam, when they become more expansive. They have a fairly limited vocabulary, tend to repeat one another's single word 'lines' and pepper their speech with **empty words** and phrases such as 'I know', 'I mean' and 'really'.

When they are with the wider group in the wood scenes they interact with the others using slightly longer phrases, but they still use simple vocabulary, and frequently ask, 'What are we going to do?' *(Three, A Wood)*.

> **empty words** words or phrases used in everyday speech as verbal 'padding' that do not communicate any meaning
>
> **monosyllable** a word made up of a single part, such as 'dead' or 'thing'

Cathy and Lou

Cathy and Lou use a restricted vocabulary and both rely on empty phrases in their speech.

Lou often uses 'bad' language, e.g. **'We are screwed'** *(One, A Wood)*, **'Oh, Jesus Christ'** *(Two, A Wood)*, **'Mark, you dick'** *(Two, A Wood)*, but otherwise her speech pattern is fairly unremarkable.

Cathy appears to be in an almost permanent state of excitement over the 'death' of Adam and she is quite boisterous in her speech, which often draws attention. As the play develops and as Cathy's love of violence increases, her need to express herself verbally wanes and, with Brian especially, she resorts to threats as well as actual blows. She also frequently uses the personal pronouns 'me' and 'I', suggesting an egotistical streak.

> **Key quotations**
>
> This is mad, eh? [...] Talk about mad. I mean, it's quite exciting as well, though, isn't it. [...] I mean I'm not saying it's a good thing, but in a way it is.
>
> *(Cathy, One, A Wood)*
>
> *(To BRIAN.)* If you don't shut up you'll be dead.
>
> *(Cathy, Three, A Wood)*
>
> *Suddenly, CATHY slaps him.*
>
> *(Cathy, Three, A Wood)*

Brian

Brian only speaks when he is highly distressed or heavily sedated and his speech reflects these states rather than signifying his social background. Kelly uses Brian's language in the scenes where he is clearly on medication to indicate how the sedatives are affecting his brain.

> **Key quotations**
>
> I crawled, I love crawling, I love crawling, Leah
>
> *(Brian, Three, A Wood)*
>
> D'you ever feel like the trees are watching you?
>
> *(Brian, Three, A Wood)*

Adam

Adam's narrative about his experience of following the tunnels out into the open is halting and fragmented, and his sentences are not fully formulated. He seems barely to recognize Leah or Phil and, although he has a strong sense of his own identity, his speech reflects a loss of both memory and language function, probably as a result of having suffered concussion or brain damage in his fall.

> **Key quotation**
>
> I live there. It's
>
> mine, I
>
> live
>
> there.
>
> Adam.
>
> *(Adam, Three, A Wood)*

Activity 5

Look carefully at the speech patterns of Adam and Brian. Write a paragraph to explain why there are some similarities between them.

Activity 6

With their permission, record two or three of your friends having a lunchtime or breaktime conversation with you, lasting about 90 seconds. Then, transcribe the words, phrases and sentences. How similar is the way you talk to your friends to the way that the group in *DNA* talk? Make a note of what is similar and what is different.

Figurative language

There is very little **figurative language** in *DNA*. The characters' language tends to be fairly literal and factual. Nevertheless, Kelly does occasionally include **imagery** and other linguistic features that are worth considering.

Violence

In her first conversation with Phil, Leah admits that she talks too much and invites Phil to punish her. She uses **hyperbole** as she suggests that Phil should 'shoot me. So kill me, Phil, call the police, lock me up, rip out my teeth with a pair of rusty pliers' *(One, A Field 1)*. Although Leah is using **irony** here, as the play develops, we learn that despite his calm exterior Phil is indeed capable of killing someone to prevent them from talking. Although Phil does not carry out the murder himself, he demonstrates it in mime to Cathy and its sole purpose is to silence Adam.

Leah also refers to her habit of talking too much as 'a crime', 'a sin', a 'catastrophe', 'stupid' and 'evil' *(One, A Field 1)*, none of which really apply to her. However, they do apply to the way Adam has been treated by the group, an incident that, at this point, Leah knows nothing about. By using these very strong words, Kelly allows the audience to think about the nature of crime and punishment.

It is also significant that, although Leah was not involved in the attack on Adam, she is capable of violent thoughts. In her next scene with Phil, she asks him what he would do 'if I killed myself, right here in front of you' and, after attempting to throttle herself, she discovers that he would do nothing *(One, A Field 2)*.

Rebirth: spiritual epiphany

Other examples of figurative language occur where a character struggles to articulate a semi-spiritual experience using literal terms. Adam, for example, describes his emergence from the tunnel that led from the grille as a birth-like experience and he uses **similes** to describe this.

> **Key quotation**
>
> crawling for a long time, I thought, but that was hard to tell, tunnels, scared, I was, I felt like the dark was my fear, do you know what I mean? I was wrapped in it. Like a soft blanket.
>
> *(Adam, Three, A Wood)*

Richard also uses similes to describe his strange experience of being in 'this big wind of fluff, like dandelions, but smaller, and tons of them, like fluffs of wool or cotton' and this sensation makes him feel 'like I was an alien in a cloud' *(Four, A Field)*. He uses another simile to describe Danny's new aversion to dentistry, telling Phil that Danny 'Can't stand the cavities, he says when they open their mouths sometimes it feels like you're going to fall in' *(Four, A Field)*, perhaps a reminder of Adam's fall through the grille.

> **figurative language** language that uses imagery and figures of speech such as similes, and is not meant to be literal
>
> **hyperbole** a form of exaggeration used in literature
>
> **imagery** visually descriptive or figurative language, which conveys ideas or emotions
>
> **irony** a technique where what is said or presented differs from what is actually meant
>
> **simile** a figure of speech that compares one thing to another using the words 'like' or 'as'

Activity 7

Open your text of *DNA* randomly and explore the lines on the double-page spread, as if it was an extract in your assessment. Pick out and comment on the effects created by the choice of monosyllabic or **polysyllabic** vocabulary and the use of the following linguistic devices:

- repetition
- hesitation or incomplete sentences
- 'bad' language or swearing
- figurative language
- direct and rhetorical questions
- personal pronouns 'I' or 'me'.

polysyllabic a word made up of more than one syllable, e.g. 'blanket' or 'dandelion'

Repetition: creating tone or atmosphere

The word that occurs more frequently than any other in *DNA* is 'dead'. It is repeated 32 times in the play. The word 'died' is used once and 'kill' appears three times. This is a short play, so Kelly's repeated use of words associated with death certainly affects its tone and makes it appear quite dark and serious.

There are also multiple references to God and Jesus. Although these references frequently take the form of an exclamation, such as Leah's repeated 'Oh my god' when she hears about the arrest of the suspect *(Two, A Wood)*, they occur frequently enough to suggest a Christian context. The words 'God', 'Jesus' or 'Christ' appear 16 times. When these words are uttered in desperation, they add to the mood of crisis that pervades the play.

There are also moments of light relief, supported by Kelly's choice of language. The character of Danny, for example, appears to be obsessed with going to 'Dental college' and becoming a dentist *(One, A Wood)*, an ambition he refers to repeatedly. It is Danny who wants to establish the state of the teeth of Adam's fictitious 'abductor', lending a slightly comical aspect to a dark situation. The group take to calling the suspect the 'postman with bad teeth' *(Two, A Field 1)*, which becomes a rather grim joke among them.

The other feature of language that creates some humour is Phil's tendency to say nothing when Leah is desperately trying to engage him in conversation. This is evident in all of their scenes set in the field, where Phil only speaks a single word to Leah and that word is 'No' *(Two, A Field 2)*. One of the moments where Phil's lack of responsiveness provokes laughter is when Leah is experiencing 'déjà vu' and predicts that he is about to 'do nothing' *(Two, A Field 2)*, a prophecy which he readily fulfils.

Although Phil only ever responds directly to Leah once, he seems to be lost when she leaves

Writing about language

Demonstrating your understanding of Kelly's use of language to imitate the way teenagers speak to one another is vital. Make sure that you have something to say about:

- Kelly's use of very short lines, monosyllabic words and repeated phrases
- his use of incomplete thought patterns, hesitations and overlapping dialogue
- the more extensive vocabulary in Leah's monologues
- the use of language to differentiate between the more and less intelligent members of the group
- Kelly's use of repeated, individual words
- his use of language of violence and cruelty.

Themes are distinct from the content of the plot but not separate from it. The plot of *DNA* deals with the aftermath of a bullying incident that led to the death of a boy. Kelly explores the complex interrelationships within the group of teenagers responsible for that death, inviting the audience to reflect on the immoral, criminal and possibly psychotic behaviour that prompted it. Introducing themes of power and rivalry, truth and lies, friendship and betrayal, guilt and responsibility, Kelly envisages a situation where getting away with murder has dreadful consequences for those involved.

Power within the group

It is useful to consider the nature of the group at the centre of the play. Far from being a teen gang that terrorizes the neighbourhood, wears distinctive clothing and engages in running battles with rival gangs, John Tate's group congregate in the woods, smoke and drink a little, and pick on weaker students. Kelly makes no reference to the exchanging of secret signs or greetings, to routine criminal activity, to the use of illegal weapons, to drug abuse or to 'turf wars'.

There is some in-fighting amongst group members. Richard and John Tate were once rivals for the leadership, which John refers to, almost fondly, as 'silliness' *(One, A Wood)*. Richard 'hates' Brian, and Danny has 'threatened to kill Cathy' *(Two, A Field 1)*. We learn that Richard and Mark have never got on, Leah reveals that she hasn't 'got friends' and Phil isn't exactly 'Mr [...] popular' *(One, A Field 1)*. The group is evidently not a group of friends. Instead, their alliance is based upon excluding others in order to protect themselves.

Kelly investigates different kinds of power relationships within the group. John Tate's power is based on intimidation tactics. He uses the threat of physical violence to control his group yet claims that his motive is to try 'to keep things together' *(One, A Wood)*. He is out of his depth once the group believes that it has hounded Adam to his death and he is forced to submit to Phil's superior intellect.

> **Key quotation**
>
> Cathy says you're clever.
>
> So. What do we do?
>
> *(John Tate, One, A Wood)*

From this point in the play, Phil assumes the role of leader and his power is not questioned. His highly developed, criminal intelligence ensures that the group evades detection and punishment for its actions. Phil leads by instruction, not by example, using his brain to control the group without personally engaging in criminal activity. However, just because Phil's power is not composed of brute force does not mean it is harmless. In a single-minded desire to finish what he started, protect the group and avoid ruin for himself and Leah, Phil makes the ruthless decision to sacrifice the outsider Adam when he reappears. Chillingly, he answers

John Tate projects a 'hard' image in the National Theatre production at the Cottesloe Theatre, 2008

Leah's objection to simply leaving Adam 'up here' with the assertive response: 'I'm in charge. Everyone is happier. What's more important; one person or everyone?' *(Three, A Wood)*.

As the drama plays out, however, and Leah leaves, Phil is left to ponder if it *is* only one person who has been sacrificed. As Richard reports, the only survivor from the attack on Adam appears to be the psychotic Cathy, who is now 'running things' *(Four, A Field)*, using violence as her means of maintaining control.

Power of bullies, peer-pressure and criminality

The bullies' torment of Adam, which leads to his horrific fall 'up the grille' *(One, A Wood)*, is graphically and memorably described by Jan and Mark in one of the most important sections of the play. Without it, the audience struggle to understand how characters like Danny, Brian and Richard can have been involved in the attack. Kelly seems to suggest that it is peer pressure and their fear of the alternative that compels these apparently 'nice' boys, and even the sensible Leah, to join the group.

The power of bullies is fuelled by the sense of security that members of the group gain from acting together and is a demonstration of herd mentality at its most dangerous. Group members appear to believe that by sticking together they normalize their criminal behaviour.

Activity 1

Although their everyday activities seem mild in comparison with hardened street gangs, John Tate's group is involved in violence, murder and a criminal cover-up. Write four paragraphs explaining whether or not you agree that Kelly is suggesting that everyone has the potential for evil. Support your ideas with evidence from the text.

Truth and lies

The group depends on a series of complicated lies fabricated by Phil and told to the authorities mainly by Richard, Brian and John Tate. Other lies are told to reporters by Cathy and, presumably, in offstage action by all of the teenagers to their parents, although this aspect of the characters' lives is never explored. Danny, Mark, Jan, Cathy and Lou all support the lies told to the authorities by carrying out Phil's practical instructions to manufacture false evidence.

There are only a handful of occasions in the play when some members of the group suggest that they ought to tell the truth about what happened to Adam. The first is when Brian, in One, shows some courage in standing up to John Tate's order to 'say nothing' *(One, A Wood)*. Despite Tate referring to him as a 'crying little piece of filth', Brian volunteers, 'I think we should tell someone' *(One, A Wood)*.

The next is in Two when Lou suggests they are 'going to have to tell them' to avoid sending the postman to jail. The final opportunity for the group to confess the truth comes when Adam is discovered. Leah's loyalty to Phil is stretched to breaking point and she tries to persuade him not to leave Adam 'here' *(Three, A Wood)*.

> **Key quotation**
>
> Let's, come on, let's, it won't be that bad, it'll be, we can explain, we can talk. We can go through the whole thing and make them understand –
> *(Leah, Three, A Wood)*

The theme of truth and lies is linked to the theme of power of course as it is the most powerful members of the group who suppress the desire of the weaker ones to seek help from the world of adults.

> **Activity 2**
>
> **a)** Phil constructs a very complicated set of lies to prevent the group from taking the blame for Adam's disappearance. Can you think of any less complicated stories they might have told to the authorities?
>
> **b)** Imagine yourself to be one of the characters from *DNA* involved in the attack on Adam. What might you have said to shift suspicion from the group?

Friendship, loyalty, sacrifice and betrayal

Kelly explores friendship and loyalty, and the related themes of betrayal and sacrifice, in *DNA*.

Jan and Mark appear to be friends from the outset and their relationship survives the crisis. Although they turn to shoplifting, their relationship is intact.

Leah talks to Phil about friendship in One and she, at least, seems to believe they've 'got each other' and that they 'need each other' *(One, A Field 1)*. Phil's desolation without Leah at the end of the play seems to support the idea that they were, indeed, boyfriend and girlfriend, and that he is lost without her.

It is Phil's sacrifice of Adam, a friend from their childhood, that finally causes Leah to see the real Phil and she **metaphorically** spits him out along with the sweet he gave her. Up to this point, she has been unswervingly loyal to him. By moving schools, 'Without saying a thing' *(Four, A Street)*, Leah puts an end to all previous friendships and starts afresh.

> **metaphorical** from 'metaphor', a comparison of one thing, idea or action to another for effect and to suggest a similarity

The others are not friends as such, although in the aftermath of Adam's death and in the absence from school of John Tate, Brian, Leah and Phil, we are told that Lou has become Cathy's 'best friend' *(Four, A Field)*.

Adam is betrayed by all the classmates who took part in goading and torturing him. His fate is sealed by surviving the ordeal and living to incriminate the others. Phil's order of execution may appear ruthless but he attempts to justify the sacrifice of Adam by posing a well-worn rhetorical question that has been applied many times in political crises, including the execution of Jesus.

> **Key quotation**
>
> What's more important; one person or everyone? *(Phil, Three, A Wood)*

> According to the Gospel of St John in the Bible (Chapter 11, verse 50), before Jesus was sentenced to death, the ruling High Priest Caiaphas advised leading Jewish figures that it would be advantageous if only one man had to die in order to save the whole nation from ruin.

Tips for assessment

You may be asked about a theme that you do not immediately recognize. For example, a question might ask you to write about the theme of authority rather than power. Always use the wording used in the question, adapting your knowledge to its precise demands.

Guilt and responsibility

At the start of the play, most of the teenagers believe they have been involved in a murder. By its close, all of them have contributed, in some way, to Adam's death.

One by one, the group members succumb to their guilt about Adam to a greater or lesser degree. John Tate is the first to withdraw from the group and drop out of school. First he refuses to 'come out of his room' *(Two, A Field 1)*, then he finds 'god'.

Brian's guilty conscience results in his mental collapse, which requires 'medication' *(Three, A Field 1)*. The more involved in criminality he becomes, the more he begins to lose touch with reality. Finally, his existence is reduced to 'drooling or giggling' *(Four, A Field)* – he is heading for an asylum.

Initially, Mark and Jan try charity work and kindness to others to help ease their guilt. This doesn't seem to help them for very long and they turn to shoplifting.

Danny is more robust. However, his guilt is shown in his sudden dislike of dentistry as the cavities in the patients' mouths seem to remind him of the grille and he feels as if he is about to 'fall in' *(Four, A Field)*.

If Phil feels guilty about his involvement in the cover-up and his order of execution on Adam, it is shown through his total withdrawal from the group. Still sitting silently in the field, he is no longer eating and simply stares into nothingness.

Richard is reduced to trying to impress Phil with his handstands. His sudden revelation about aliens suggests that, like Brian, his involvement in the cover-up may be causing him to start losing his grip on reality.

Cathy's involvement in the bullying and murder of Adam has sharpened her appetite for further violence. She showed no conscience about putting an innocent man behind bars. Completely without a moral compass, Cathy ends the play terrorizing the younger pupils at school with Lou as her sidekick.

Leah appears to have less to be guilty about than any of the others, having had nothing to do with the bullying incident and not having taken an active part in the cover-up. She begs Phil not to harm Adam but she fails to stop him. She also has to face up to the guilt of having practically worshipped a

Richard tries to get Phil to respond and return to the group

boy who turns out to have psychopathic tendencies. The strongest character in the play, Leah moves schools and removes herself from the influence of the rest of the group. She is a survivor.

Activity 3

Kelly is on record as saying that the characters in *DNA* know the difference between right and wrong.

a) Find reasons for and against the idea that Kelly is using the play to teach a moral lesson.

b) Develop your ideas into a more detailed essay plan, using textual support for your argument.

Other related themes

Kelly explores the nature of criminality, severely mentally ill behaviour and ostracism (exclusion from a group) in the course of the unfolding plot, inviting us to consider the health of a society represented, in miniature, in the teenage group led by John Tate.

Other related themes include cause and effect, speech and silence, individual choice and free will, the nature of being human, right and wrong/ good and evil, and religion.

Writing about themes

You may be asked to write about an individual theme or a pair of themes. There are different ways that such questions might be asked. You might be asked how Kelly presents a theme, for example:

> How does Kelly present the theme of power in *DNA*?

This type of question requires you to consider the different methods the playwright uses to convey this theme. Alternatively, you might be asked to consider the relative importance of a theme, for example:

> How important do you think the themes of truth and lies are in the play?

> How far do you consider the play to be about loyalty and betrayal?

To answer this type of question, you should consider how the themes relate to Kelly's main purpose and message, and how they compare to other significant themes.

The performance of a play can only be achieved through collaboration between a director and a cast of actors, supported by a design team responsible for setting and costume, lighting and sound. The members of such a production team all work together on the playwright's script to find ways to bring the play to life for an audience.

The play in production

It is the role of the director to interpret the play and to share that interpretation with the cast so that the production the audience sees represents one person's vision of the play.

Because *DNA* was first produced for the Connections Festival by amateur youth groups, there were numerous 'first' productions being rehearsed all at the same time, each led or directed by different youth leaders or drama teachers. This resulted in many different interpretations of the play being performed in different venues up and down the country. No two productions of any play are exactly the same, but the differences between the Connections Festival productions of *DNA* were especially pronounced because of Kelly's decision to open the play up to all actors, in terms of gender and ethnicity. He did this by inserting this message before the play text, following the list of characters: 'Names and genders of characters are suggestions only, and can be changed to suit performers'. Consequently, groups were free to present an all-male or all-female cast, for example, or to switch the genders of the main characters.

There have only been two professional productions of *DNA* since the Connections Festival in 2007. The first professional production of the play was by the National Theatre, presented at the Cottesloe Theatre, London in 2008. It was directed by Paul Miller, with a cast of young professional actors including Sam Crane and Ruby Bentall as Phil and Leah. The second was a touring production in 2012, staged by the Hull Truck Theatre Company and directed by Anthony Banks. It was performed in theatres in 20 venues around the country, over a six-month period. James Alexandrou played Phil and Leah Brotherhead played Leah. Both of these productions followed Kelly's original casting in terms of characters' names and genders.

Tips for assessment

For the purposes of the assessment, although you might wish to make the point that Kelly has opened the play up to a variety of casting possibilities, you should write about the characters as originally envisaged by Kelly.

Director's role: casting the actors

The director reads and re-reads the script many times before making crucial decisions about the production and what they want the audience to experience and take away from it. For example, should an audience at a performance of *DNA* leave the theatre thinking about changing a society where school-age children can get away with murder or should they be moved, instead, to think about the consequences of their own actions and small, random acts of cruelty or selfishness? Only once the director has decided on the effects they wish to create for the audience can work on the play begin in earnest.

At this point, the director has to give a great deal of thought to the casting of the roles. Casting is vitally important in determining the way an audience reacts to each individual character, often affecting the way the audience responds to the whole play. For example, casting Phil as a stereotypical hero figure (tall, handsome and silent) or as something of a 'nerd' whose brains alone turn him into the leader that the group needs, will affect the way the audience understands the whole play.

Activity 1

Write two paragraphs explaining what you think Phil should look and sound like. Make sure that your ideas are justified with reference to the text of the play.

The director selects an actor for each role in the play, taking into account each actor's physical appearance in terms of their age, build, height, colouring, facial features and vocal qualities. In this way, the director tries to create a whole ensemble of actors most likely to deliver his/her vision of the play. A director of *DNA* is in the unusual position of needing to cast professional actors, each with a **playing age** of around 15–16 years old, in order to be able to convince the audience of the characters' lack of maturity. For example, in the Hull Truck production, the role of Phil was played by 27-year-old James Alexandrou, with a playing age considered to be 15–30.

playing age the age range that an actor is capable of portraying on stage

Activity 2

Imagine you are going to be directing a production of *DNA*. Write down the physical and vocal qualities you would be looking for in the actors you cast to play the roles of Leah, Brian, Richard, Adam and Cathy. Justify your decisions by referring closely to the text.

Performers

Having selected the appropriate actor for each role, in terms of their appearance and vocal qualities, the director must work with them to help them develop their character. With a play like *DNA*, where many of the characters are relatively sketchily drawn and where the playwright offers no guidance about their appearance or background, this is a major task. The director will decide, for example, how sympathetic Phil should appear to the audience. Phil says so little in the play that the director will need to make sure that the actor is constantly 'performing' when on stage, listening and responding – or consciously not responding – to what the others, especially Leah, have to say. The actor playing Phil must absorb the director's vision for the role and translate it into a believable character.

Most of the characters show a range of emotions throughout the play but they express these emotions, as we have seen, using short, often repetitive and unfinished lines of text. The meaning and emotion behind these half-lines and incomplete utterances must be conveyed in the theatre through facial expression, body language, spatial relationships on stage and other forms of non-verbal communication.

When we read the play we have to imagine the actors' tone of voice, movement, gesture and handling of **props** whereas, when we are watching a production, the actors demonstrate all of these aspects in their performances.

The non-verbal reactions of the group are especially useful in conveying to the audience their shock at the unfolding events as well as the subtle shifts in the moods of individuals and the relationships between group members.

props moveable objects used on stage by the actors

Activity 3

Add to the examples of non-verbal communication in the play in the table opposite by looking at each of the sequences that take place in the wood. Make sure to link your ideas to the text and explain what the non-verbal reactions are intended to convey.

Type of non-verbal communication	Potential examples from *DNA*
Use of space	Moving closer to another character to show: • intimacy (Leah sits by Phil) • confrontation (Richard steps closer to John Tate) • intimidation (John Tate walks towards Brian) • false friendship (Phil goes to Lou to reassure her). Retreating/moving away to show: • disengagement (Phil just walks off after ordering Adam's execution) • disillusion (Leah storms off after Phil's instructions to Cathy).
Use of pause, beat, silence	To show: • control (Phil's power over Leah) • tension (John's threat to 'hurt' Richard) • confusion (Adam in his monologue) • awkwardness (during Leah's monologues).
Eye contact; eyeline	To show: • shock or amazement (the group stare after Phil explains his plan) • fear (Brian looks up to suggest telling someone) • admiration (Leah stares at Phil) • anger and disappointment (Leah glares at Phil).
Facial expression	To show: • glee or hysteria (Cathy grinning).
Body language	To show: • support, not necessarily genuine (Phil nods at Brian) • willing involvement (Jan nods to Mark after Adam is led away) • disgust (Leah spits out the sweet).
Tears/laughter	To show: • misery/guilt (Brian crying) • despair (Leah crying) • hysteria/mental affliction (Brian giggling).
Physical contact	To show: • friendship/support, not necessarily genuine (Phil lays a hand on Brian's shoulder) • understanding/comfort, not necessarily genuine (Phil puts his arm around Leah).
Use of props	To show: • boredom/indifference (Phil eats junk food) • obsession (Phil prepares a waffle) • bewilderment (Leah displays Jerry in a Tupperware box).

Stage setting

A stage designer works closely with the director to achieve the setting that the director wants and/or that the playwright stipulates. In the case of *DNA*, the settings comprise a street, a field and a wood. While it is possible to create a realistic representation of each of these locations in modern theatres in order to give the illusion of the outdoors on stage, it is not really practical. In a play that lasts just over an hour and that returns to the 'field' seven times in all, alternating with scenes set in the street and the wood, most designers would be tempted to adopt a pragmatic approach to signalling the changing locations.

Both stage designers associated with the professional productions of *DNA* – Simon Daw at the Cottesloe and Anthony Banks for the Hull Truck tour – chose to use a more or less bare stage, flooded with atmospheric lighting, and projections of the outside world to suggest the shifts in location.

Simon Daw's design consisted of a bare open stage with a visible **lighting rig**, which was capable of changing the mood on stage in an instant, washing it in different, intense hues. Behind the action was a full height **cyclorama** on which were projected images of the different locations. Most impressive of all was the midnight-blue image of woodland in twilight, which dominated the screen, dwarfing the actors and seemingly amplifying their inexperience and inability to cope with the situation that they had unwittingly created.

Simon Daw's wood set at the Cottesloe Theatre, London, 2008

cyclorama a cloth or screen stretched tight in an arc around the back of a stage set and used for projections and/or multi-media images

lighting rig a bar or set of bars from which stage lanterns and special lights are suspended; they may be concealed but are often exposed

Anthony Banks directed and designed the production for the Hull Truck tour. Like Daw, he adopted quite a minimalist approach to staging and used projections and sound to signal scene changes. The back 'wall' was created out of plastic strips, like vertical blinds, upon which the various locations were projected. The characters made their entrances and exits through these strips as if emerging from gaps between the trees in the wood. The only additional part of the set was created by a floor cloth that resembled artificial grass and provided the seating area when Phil and Leah were in the field. The street scene was represented as if viewed from the top of a bus or train with Jan and Mark communicating on mobile phones.

Activity 4

Imagine you have been asked to design a set for your school's production of *DNA*. How might you present the different settings and execute the scene changes between them?

Anthony Banks's wood set for the Hull Truck Theatre Company production in 2012

Costume

In the production of most plays, costume design is a vital tool in conveying information to the audience about the period setting of the play, the relative ages and/or status of the characters, their professions and individual styles.

In *DNA*, the whole cast plays school pupils. They are all in their mid-teens. Although each has their place in the group hierarchy, they are all more or less equal socially. In most productions, amateur and professional, the costumes consist of school uniforms in varying degrees of tidiness and conformity. In the National Theatre production, almost all the cast wore school shirts and ties with dark trousers or skirts and various types of jacket including school blazers, hoodies and anoraks. The Hull Truck production used more varied costumes, with basic school uniforms plus non-uniform-style jackets, hats and trainers.

Activity 5

Even school uniform can be worn distinctively by different characters in the play to reflect their characters. Decide on a uniform for the characters and choose some accessories to make each character look slightly different. Base your decisions for the designs on the characters' personalities as revealed in the play.

Props

There are very few props necessary in *DNA* and none of them demands elaborate design.

- Phil requires a variety of props, most of which are snacks: ice cream; a can or bottle of Coke; a bag of crisps; a packet of Starburst or Toffo; a muffin or pie; a plastic bag containing a paper plate, a waffle, butter, jam, and a knife, and large enough to be used to suffocate Adam.
- Leah requires a suitcase and a Tupperware container with something inside it that resembles a dead hamster or guinea pig.
- Brian requires some earth to eat.

Lighting and sound

Theatre technology is very sophisticated and, in addition to illuminating the action, lighting can create effects very similar to natural daylight, sunlight or moonlight, if required. Lighting and sound can be combined to suggest a busy street, with the sound of people chatting, heels walking on pavements, the sound of traffic and the occasional car horn, all of which can create the sense of a public space. For a field, tranquility can be created through projections of clouds moving across 'sky' on the cyclorama and recorded birdsong can add to the mood and sense of remoteness. For woods, lighting can be used to suggest light streaming through the trees. More sound effects of birds or even a babbling brook will give the sense of a natural hideaway.

In the professional productions of *DNA*, the directors commissioned sound designers Rich Walsh at the Cottesloe and Alex Baronowski for the Hull Truck tour to create an edgy musical soundtrack to introduce each show and cover the transitions, creating distinctive moods and atmospheres for the play's ever-darkening tone.

Of course, the play is open to any number of design interpretations and the designer of a future production might decide to have more elaborate, naturalistic settings. A set designer might choose, for example, to create some kind of hideaway in the wood for the group, with seating and other things the group have accumulated. A costume designer might design a wider range of costumes to reflect meetings between the group at weekends or in the evenings after school as well as on schooldays. (There is only one reference in the play, made by Richard, to having come directly from school.) Similarly, the characters could have more props than they require, including mobile phones and other gadgets, bags or books, for example. There are endless possibilities.

Activity 6

You can access photographs and reviews of the two professional productions on the Internet. There are also numerous full-length amateur/school productions of *DNA*, as well as edited highlights, on YouTube, which may give you further ideas about how the play might be designed. Spend some time reviewing clips of student performances and productions, and make a list of the different design choices that have been made.

Writing about performance

Remember to write about Kelly's intentions for the audience rather than the reader, as it is the audience that the playwright is addressing. Even if you do not have an opportunity to see the play at the theatre, you need to imagine what the scenes would look like on stage as well as the effects that are created for the audience as the action unfolds.

Remember that assessment questions are based on the text as Kelly wrote it and characters' names and genders will be assumed to be those published in the cast list. You should avoid referring to productions you have seen or performed in where genders and names have been changed to suit the cast.

Exam skills

Make sure you are fully prepared for the challenges of the assessment by following these practical steps.

Step 1: Make sure you know the play really well

DNA is a very short play, but its structure and plot demand careful attention. Try to read it at least four times and listen to or watch good versions that are available on the Internet. As you re-read the play, make your own notes under the following headings:

- Plot and structure
- Language
- Context
- Themes
- Characters
- Performance.

Step 2: Revise thoroughly

Go back through this book and check that you have completed all the activities. Re-read the key quotations from the play that appear throughout this book and try to learn as many as you can.

Practise analysing extracts. For example, open the play randomly at any page and write at least one paragraph about the significance of the contents of the page in relation to the list of bullet points in Step 1.

Choose one of the characters from the play to focus on. Practise writing a page or more about how Kelly presents that character and how they function in the play. Repeat the task for the other characters.

Choose one of the following themes and practise writing a page or more about its importance in the play: power, violence, truth and lies, loyalty and betrayal. Repeat the task for other themes.

Activity 1

Look back through the pages you have written about themes and characters. Find relevant quotations from the play to help support your ideas.

Step 3: Improve your exam technique

If you are sitting an exam on your set text, brushing up on exam technique is really worth the effort and can make a real difference to your overall grade. Opposite are examples of the different question types you may be faced with in your exam.

Make sure you know which type of question you will face in your assessment – essay-style questions or extract-based questions.

Essay-style questions

Most essay-style questions ask you to write about the plot (the events that take place in the play), the structure (how events are organized), the characters or the themes. Below are some typical essay-style questions. The key words and phrases are underlined, followed by a brief explanation of what each question requires.

> <u>How</u> does <u>Kelly</u> present <u>Leah</u> in the play?

This question is about character. The 'how' part refers to Kelly's methods for creating character, which might include:

- what the character looks and sounds like
- what the character says about himself/herself and others
- how the character interacts with various other characters
- how the character may be compared/contrasted with other characters
- what the character does – his/her actions and/or reactions in the play
- what kind of language the character uses when speaking.

> <u>How</u> is the <u>theme of loyalty</u> presented in *DNA*?

This question is about theme. The 'how' part refers to the methods the playwright uses to convey this theme.

> *DNA* has been described <u>as a play about choices</u>. <u>How far do you agree</u> with this description?

This question is about the nature of the play as a whole. 'How far do you agree?' means that you should weigh up the evidence for agreeing (or disagreeing) with the description and provide evidence to support your views. A good way to approach this type of question is to consider the appropriateness of the statement in relation to plot, structure, characters, themes, mood/atmosphere and language.

Extract-based questions

For extract-based questions you should look at past paper or specimen paper questions to familiarize yourself with the precise demands of the type of question that is specific to the exam you are going to take. You will need to have plenty of practice in reading extracts carefully, paying close attention to language as well as to the action that occurs in the extract.

When writing extract-based answers, use a pen or highlighter to underline key words/phrases in the extract that strike you as important. It can also be helpful to make brief notes in the margin to remind you why you chose those phrases.

Step 4: Answer the question

Always think ahead and plan before you start writing. This will help you to:

- structure your answer logically
- target the precise demands of the question
- avoid missing out points that are crucial to your argument
- include appropriate quotations.

Plans may take a number of forms. However, a brief list is often the most helpful as it allows you to put your ideas into a logical sequence. In an exam, you need to plan quickly. Don't spend more than about six or seven minutes on a plan before you start writing.

Develop your answer step by step, building your argument by referring to precise moments from the extract or wider play. Always support your answer with short, relevant quotations from the play.

The most effective way to use a quotation is to absorb it into your own sentences, for example:

> In the third scene set in the woods, Kelly presents Adam as a 'boy who looks like a tramp'. He is utterly bewildered, surrounded by the others in the group and looking at them as though they were 'Aliens' (Three, A Wood).
>
> This is a turning point in the play as Phil realizes immediately that if Adam comes back, 'our lives are ruined' (Three, A Wood).

Sample questions

1

In *DNA*, Leah tells Phil, 'You're a miracle worker', referring to the way the group has been transformed by his leadership. How far do you agree with Leah's assessment?

Write about:

- how Kelly presents Phil's 'transformation' of the group
- how Kelly uses the character of Phil to explore ideas about the criminal mind.

2

Consider the significance of the three different settings in *DNA*. In what ways is each setting appropriate to the action that takes place there?

Write about:

- how Kelly uses the different settings for different types of activity
- why Jan and Mark are the only characters to appear in all three settings.

3

Kelly has been quoted as saying that the characters in *DNA* know the difference between right and wrong. Choose two characters and explore Kelly's presentation of their contrasting attitudes to the wrong things that they are doing.

Write about:

- how Kelly presents characters' attitudes to their actions and reactions
- how these attitudes are shown to be contrasting.

4

How does Kelly present the theme of responsibility in *DNA*?

Write about:

- how Kelly presents the theme through his creation of character
- how the theme develops as the plot progresses.

5

Kelly presents two victim figures in *DNA* – Adam and Brian. What methods does Kelly use to create sympathy for these two characters?

Write about:

- how Kelly presents the characters of Adam and Brian
- how their characterization invites sympathy.

6

Kelly attempts to recreate the speech rhythms and patterns of contemporary teenagers in *DNA*. How does he achieve this? Give examples from the play and consider how far he is successful.

Write about:

- Kelly's use of language in the play, including the vocabulary as well as the structure of the characters' speeches
- how successful you think he is.

Sample answers

Sample answer 1

In *DNA*, Cathy says, 'I mean I'm not saying it's a good thing, but in a way it is.' How does Kelly present Cathy in the play?

Write about:

- how Kelly presents the character of Cathy
- how Kelly uses the character of Cathy to explore ideas about good and evil.

In 'DNA', Kelly presents Cathy as the most unpredictable group member, who does not react to Adam's death in the same way as the other teenagers. When she enters the play, John Tate is trying to calm down Lou and Danny, who are agitated and afraid of the consequences of their actions. Cathy is described as 'grinning' and the fact that Kelly has her arriving with Brian, who is 'crying', highlights the contrast between them and emphasizes how inappropriate Cathy's response to Adam's death is. This is the first time Kelly suggests a contrast between good and evil.

Makes a purposeful opening to the answer, showing understanding of Cathy's character.

Rather than helping John Tate to 'keep things together', Cathy delights in causing trouble amongst the other group members. Sensing a rift between John and Danny, she insists, 'He's on Richard's side,' and then she repeats the idea, emphatically stating, 'He is'. In this way, Kelly presents Cathy as disruptive and a negative influence on the potential harmony of the group. She appears to have no sense of the magnitude of what they, as a group, have done.

Gives a useful sense of Cathy's character but could be more focused on her response to Adam's death.

Kelly presents Cathy as fearless in her willingness to carry out her part in the cover-up. The tasks Phil makes her do are risky, involving breaking and entering at Adam's house and taking DNA from a random stranger.

Although Cathy is not alone in being prepared to go to extreme lengths to avoid being blamed for Adam's death, she appears to be the most enthusiastic. Kelly reveals that, by framing an actual postal worker for Adam's disappearance, Cathy does not fully understand the job she has been asked to do. It also shows that she does not care about an innocent person being jailed for a crime that she committed and that he had no involvement in. Through Cathy's indifference, contrasted with the anguish of other group members, Kelly is conveying to the audience that this is an evil act.

Makes a better point of reference which looks at Cathy's lack of a sense of responsibility for Adam's death.

The language Kelly gives Cathy to speak shows her to be self-obsessed and that she displays an inappropriate response to Adam's death. Initially she refers to the situation as 'mad', a term that appears woefully inadequate to sum up the death of a classmate after a session of systematic cruelty. Cathy also describes the situation as 'quite exciting as well'. Her ability

Gives some useful analysis of Kelly's choice of language for Cathy.

Uses text, again, to support the developing argument.

to distance herself from the person that she knew and to focus on the 'excitement' of an event that she describes as 'Better than ordinary life' hints at an abnormal personality, which might be compared to that of a sociopath.

Focuses well on both prongs of the question.

Later, when the poor postman is arrested, Cathy is presented as being almost intoxicated by her involvement in the case and the fact that reporters want to interview her. She intends to go back when she has time and even ask for money. Her eagerness to profit from Adam's death is particularly sickening and Kelly asks his audience to reflect on the nature of true evil.

Another way in which Kelly presents Cathy's response to Adam's death is through her increased reliance on threats and violence to get what she wants. Having discovered that they can actually kill a classmate and suffer no repercussions, Cathy enters a spiral of increasingly vicious behaviour.

Makes helpful reference to what Cathy says and to what the audience sees her do.

In Three, Brian tells the others that Cathy 'loves violence now' and we hear from Cathy herself that she threatened to 'gouge one of' Adam's eyes out to force him to come out of his hideout in the hedge. This shows that, far from being relieved to find Adam alive, she reacts unpredictably and inappropriately to his reappearance. Further episodes of unpredictability can be seen when Cathy slaps Brian suddenly and for no apparent reason and, later in the same scene, Kelly shows her threatening Brian, 'If you don't shut up you'll be dead'.

Towards the end of the play, Richard reports to Phil on Cathy's decline into completely evil behaviour when he describes her 'running things' in school. Her reign of terror appears to have no limits as she is said to have 'cut a first year's finger off'.

The report of what Cathy has become is also well focused and useful.

Cathy's response to Adam's initial 'death' and to his return is entirely self-interested. She appears to enjoy the publicity of his disappearance at the beginning of the play and becomes the willing tool of Phil in Adam's cold-blooded execution at the end. Her lust for power and violence propels her into the leadership position that Phil and John Tate previously occupied. Unlike these two figures, however, Cathy has no concern at all for the welfare of the group and she ends the play well on the way to a life of evil behaviour.

This is a fluent and focused response to the question with appropriate attention paid both to Kelly's methods of presenting Cathy and to her tendency for evil. Although there is little reference to 'good' in the answer, this is perhaps understandable given the focus on the character of Cathy.

Sample answer 2

> What effects do you think Kelly intends by setting the action of *DNA* in different outdoor settings?
>
> Write about:
>
> - how the action is divided between the street, the field and the woods
> - the effects created by these different settings.

Kelly has chosen to divide up the action of this short play into 14 even shorter 'scenes' and to follow the characters as some of them troop from school to the streets (Jan and Mark), to a field (Leah and Phil) and to the woods (all the characters at some point or other).

Focuses well on the question and Kelly's intentions.

The play deals exclusively with the experiences of teenagers in today's society and this particular group seems to spend most of their free time outside, in the fresh air, rather than hunched over computer screens. Kelly sets the action of the play outdoors because this is where John Tate's gang hangs out. They don't loiter around the school that they go to and they don't appear to meet up in each other's houses. They stay well away from their parents and their teachers. Instead, they 'get up to no good' in the freedom of the outdoors, on the street, in a field and especially in the woods.

Makes fair observation but it would be helped by some textual support.

The woods, where the whole gang meet up, is the main setting for the action. John Tate boasts to Danny and Lou in the first scene set in the woods, 'Doesn't everyone want to be us, come here in the woods? Isn't that worth keeping hold of?' John Tate appears to be proud of the gang's territory and he suggests that it is the envy of others in the school.

Supports the point well with quotation.

Woods are often seen, in literature and legend, as dangerous places where all kinds of mischief takes place. In children's stories like 'Little Red Riding Hood' and 'Hansel and Gretel' as well as in adult literature such as Shakespeare's 'A Midsummer Night's Dream', a woodland setting suggests a place of danger and unpredictability. The same effects are achieved by Kelly in his scenes set in the woods.

Shows good understanding of the broader implications of the setting.

In psychological terms, the woods may represent a place where characters are free from the restraints of society. Certainly John Tate's gang does not appear to be pestered by any outsiders as they make their plans, drinking and smoking, away from the reach of adult authority. Only when Adam makes an unwelcome appearance, 'sort of hanging around' and 'trying to be part of' the gang, are they troubled by intrusion and they soon find a way of getting rid of him.

Uses text to support an inference about how Adam got himself into trouble with the group.

The woods are the gang's headquarters. Initially, it is John Tate who is in charge of his little band of 'outlaws', but when the gravity of the situation that they are in finally dawns on him, he readily hands over the reins of power to Phil.

Phil is equally at home in the field or the woods, provided that he has his snacks with him. In his first appearance in the woods, he seems to fuel his brain with an innocent swig of Coke. Surrounded by the woods, Phil gets the inspiration for his cover-up plan, which involves footprints in the mud, an old jumper of Adam's caught on a hedge and, most importantly, a fictitious 'flasher', who would plausibly take to the woods as a place where he can show 'his willy' to the first unsuspecting victim he comes across. One effect of setting this scene in the woods, then, is to prompt Phil to think of his plan. Phil exploits the reputation of the woods as a place where 'dodgy' people hang around to create a believable alternative version of what happened to Adam when he dared to invade the territory of the John Tate gang.

Shows a thoughtful approach to the question.

Makes a fair point, although it may be time to move on to the other settings.

The woods are not Phil's favourite outdoor haunt. He and Leah appear to prefer the peace and quiet of the field for their regular meetings, suggesting that they have a personal relationship that is more important to them than their gang membership.

Makes a reasonable assumption but it should be supported from the text.

The precise nature of the field is never defined by Kelly. It doesn't appear to be particularly remote, since it is evidently accessible to Jan and Mark, who frequently leave the street to interrupt Leah and Phil in their special space and to summon them to a pow-wow in the woods. In the final scene, Richard joins Phil in the field, instead of Leah. Although he refers to the field as being 'up here', suggesting a hill, perhaps, there is no real sense of it being far away from either of the other locations.

The field is important because it is where Phil and Leah go away from the others and so Kelly creates the effect of them having a special relationship.

Remains focused on Kelly's intended effects.

The street setting is an urban space and more fitting for Jan and Mark's fairly mindless exchange of gossip.

This is an insightful response but it does not use Kelly's text enough to support the points made. There is certainly an understanding of the purpose of these settings, however, and how they accommodate some of the action. There are intelligent comments about the symbolism of the woods as well as the practical function of the location.

Sample answer 3

In *DNA*, Kelly explores ideas about an individual's responsibility in society. How does he convey this theme to his audience?

Write about:

- how Kelly presents the theme of responsibility in society
- how Kelly uses different characters to explore this theme.

Because 'DNA' is a drama, rather than a lecture, Kelly has to use different characters to represent different attitudes towards social responsibility.

Clearly focuses on the question.

There are a number of occasions in the play where it looks as if what Kelly is really interested in is what makes a healthy society. A healthy society is founded on individuals who all accept responsibility for the good of everyone.

Gives a useful definition, showing understanding of what the question requires.

In the first wood scene, John Tate initially appears to feel responsible for 'trying to keep things together' and by 'things' he appears to refer to the group that he leads.

At first, he has only Danny and Lou to consider, as they are panicking about what has happened to Adam and how it will affect them. John puts forward a rational suggestion based on the assumption that his group is a fully functioning society. He appeals to them: 'Look, we have to keep together. We have to trust each other and believe in each other.' These sound like ideal beliefs for a group leader to have. Unfortunately, once John is challenged, he demonstrates that he is unable to follow his own ideals. He does not 'trust' Richard; he fears him as a competitor. He does not 'believe in' Brian, as he refers to him as a 'crying little piece of filth'.

A very good section with excellent textual support.

Listening to Jan and Mark's description of what the group did to Adam, John Tate comes to the realization that perhaps he doesn't have the power to protect his group from the consequences of their actions. He gives up his responsibility for their welfare to the cleverer Phil.

This is ironic, as Leah has just been attempting to protect Phil from John's anger, assuming that they have been summoned by John to be called to account for some wrong-doing by Phil: 'if you're thinking it might just have been him, on his own, without me, well that's not, we are completely, I am responsible as much as he, as much as Phil'. This shows Leah's willingness to shoulder responsibility, even for something that she has not done. Leah conveys some of Kelly's ideas about responsible societies when she talks to Phil about the difference between chimpanzees and bonobos.

Still focuses and links closely to the text.

Gives a good example and focuses on Kelly's methods.

With the account of Adam's hideous death fresh in her mind, she explains that 'Chimps are evil' and talks about how any chimp can find himself 'outside of a group' and being 'hounded to death by the others'. She also points out that bonobos, unlike chimps, have 'Empathy', and it is actually empathy that makes for a successful and harmonious society of responsible individuals.

Once Phil's plan is put into operation, even though Leah has no role in it, and had no role in the death of Adam, she still assumes responsibility. She continues to identify with the group's difficulties and uses the personal pronoun 'we' to describe the actions of the group. For example, when the postman is arrested, she says, 'we made that description up', even though the description was made up by Phil. Later she begs Phil not to leave Adam in the hedge but to get help for him: 'he's insane Phil, he needs help'. Leah is willing to take responsibility for Adam and pleads with Phil to come clean over Adam's disappearance:

'LEAH: We can't leave him here, I mean that's not, are you serious? Are you seriously –

Alright, yes, there'll be –

Phil, this is insane. I mean I've never, but this, because, alright, whatever, but this is actually insane.'

Phil's response is an emphatic negative. He even quotes back to Leah something that she said to him earlier and he justifies his wrong-doing by claiming that he has more of a responsibility to the group than to 'singular' Adam: 'I'm in charge. Everyone is happier. What's more important; one person or everyone?'

Ultimately, Leah shows that she is prepared to take responsibility for her own destiny. She has tried and failed to moderate Phil's nihilistic view on life, she has lost her self-respect and betrayed her better instincts in allowing Phil to have Adam murdered. Uncharacteristically, 'Without saying a thing', Leah moves school and leaves the flawed society she used to belong to behind her.

Kelly has created, in Leah, a responsible member of society, for whom the audience feels empathy and we applaud her decision to leave the group and its chimp-like behaviours behind her.

Good attention to language.

Maintains the focus.

Confidently comments on and analyses Leah.

This is a very assured piece of work that remains consistently focused on the demands of the question. It is well argued and well supported. There is evident understanding of some of Kelly's messages as well as his methods. Three characters are considered in this extract from the answer, representing a good range of ideas.

Sample answer 4

> Explore how Kelly presents group dynamics in the extract from John Tate's line, 'I'm gonna, I'm gonna hurt you, actually' to Danny's, 'I'm not!' *(One, A Wood)*.
>
> Write about:
>
> - the relationship between John Tate and Richard at the beginning of the extract
> - the fear of John Tate felt by the rest of the group
> - Kelly's creation of growing tension.

The extract comes at a crucial point in the play when John Tate feels threatened and under pressure. He has just banned Lou and Danny from saying the word 'dead' as it reminds him of the brutal bullying of Adam that he no doubt had a leading role in.

Although everyone in the group knows that John Tate is the boss, they are more afraid now about what the police might do to them for causing Adam's death than they are about John's threats. This makes them jittery.

Gives a useful context but makes points that are not supported.

Richard was not present when John Tate banned the word 'dead' so he is not challenging John when he says it. Nevertheless, John just flips and threatens to 'hurt' Richard. He has chosen the wrong person to threaten because Richard is a grounded individual who won't take any nonsense, and he answers John back. While John Tate uses the colloquial phrases 'I'm gonna' and 'I'm gonna hurt you, actually', Richard shows his superiority over Tate by replying using Standard English, questioning Tate in an incredulous tone, 'You're going to hurt me?'

Useful focus on language.

The group dynamic shifts here as the onlookers, Cathy, Lou and Danny, are impressed by Richard's bravery in taking on the boss and also fearful in case the situation escalates and involves them. I expect they are holding their breaths.

Refers to group dynamics, one focus of the question.

Richard could say his line in various ways. He could emphasize the words 'you're' and 'me', trying to make Tate look small in front of the others, or he could emphasize the word 'hurt' as if scared of Tate. If he emphasizes the fact that he has corrected Tate's pronunciation of 'going to', that could also cause more friction between them. Either way, it is a tense moment.

Gives some sense of drama.

While Tate and Richard lock horns, with Richard repeating 'Me?' and Tate sticking to his guns and saying, 'Yes. If you use that word', stupid Cathy is still wittering on about how exciting it all is. In the group dynamic, she is on the outside, in her own bubble and completely unaware of how much trouble she is in.

Uses a rather colloquial expression.

Because Danny thinks little of Cathy and possibly because he wants to focus on the show-down between Tate and Richard, Danny tells Cathy to 'Shut up'. She retaliates with her own unimaginative retort, 'You shut up', which shows how the group is often divided, with conflict and squabbling among members a common event.

Good attention to how dynamics are shown.

John Tate ignores the scrap and pursues his own agenda, which is to try to restore some harmony in the group. He tells Richard principally, but also with a view to calming everyone down, 'I am trying to keep everyone together', and he reminds them of how much they have benefited from having him as their leader, ending his little speech by asking them to reflect, 'Isn't that worth keeping hold of?'

Instead of a resounding cheer, the group fall silent and there is an awkward moment. The group dynamics swing against John, and Richard continues to pressurize him, saying,'You shouldn't threaten me, John'. John begins to lose his nerve and, not to lose face in front of the group, he takes umbrage with Richard, asking him aggressively, 'I beg your pardon' as if he cannot believe his own ears. Richard is not prepared to back down and tension begins to rise as he repeats, 'you shouldn't threaten me' twice.

Maintains focus on tension.

John Tate is on the back foot, but he calls Richard's bluff, demanding 'Or what?' and waiting to see if Richard will finally give in. If John Tate has aggressive body language at this point it might account for Richard's hesitance as he begins to falter saying only, 'Well...', a line which trails away.

Suddenly the group dynamic shifts as Danny weighs in on Richard's behalf. Trying to placate John, he suggests that Richard is 'just saying', which brings John Tate to a nasty accusation, 'Are you on his side, Danny?'

Confidently comments and analyses.

While Danny vigorously denies being on Richard's side, Cathy, sensing some more excitement, joins in to goad Danny, insisting to John Tate that Danny is on 'Richard's side'. On stage, the group probably shifts position as Danny is keen to distance himself from Richard all of a sudden, emphatically contradicting Cathy's malicious suggestion with a definite 'I'm not!'

The scene is now set for a major readjustment of allegiances; John Tate looks weak and both Danny and Richard are in trouble. Kelly has shown the group dynamic to be shifting and it is only a matter of time before John Tate loses his role of leader and leaves the play.

This response works through the extract chronologically and frequently refers to the group and to tension. Less detail is offered on the group's fear of John Tate. Sometimes the expression is a little casual but there are several good insights, although they are not always supported from the text.

Glossary

allegorical having a spiritual, moral or political meaning clearly symbolic of something else

catalyst something that brings about a change of direction in the story

choric ode in ancient Greek theatre, a section of text delivered by the Chorus directly to the audience

Chorus a group in a Greek tragedy that commented in unison on the action of the play

circumstantial evidence evidence that suggests that someone might be guilty but which is not conclusive

classical literature literature from ancient Greece and Rome

cliff-hanger a tense and exciting ending to an episode

climax the highest or most intense part of a literary work

colloquial speech conversational language

complication or **reversal** the part of a literary work that occurs when the main character's progress is complicated, reversed or threatened

cyclorama a cloth or screen stretched tight in an arc around the back of a stage set and used for projections and/or multi-media images

denouement the resolution of the plot of a literary work

dialogue speech between any number of characters

duologue speech between two characters

empty words words or phrases used in everyday speech as verbal 'padding' that do not communicate any meaning

epiphany a moment when someone suddenly sees or understands something in a new or very clear way

episode a section of action or dialogue between two or three actors that advances the plot of a play and drives the action forward

exposition the part of a literary work that gives key information about the setting, characters and situation to help the audience make sense of it

external structure the way a piece of literature is divided into sections

fatalism a belief that man does not have the free will to change what has already been 'mapped out'

figurative language language that uses imagery and figures of speech such as similes, and is not meant to be literal

foil a character that contrasts with another in order to show up certain qualities or failings

grammatical construction the way language is conventionally arranged into units to form sentences, made up of nouns, verbs, prepositions, conjunctions, adjectives and/or adverbs

group dynamic the inter-relationships between a group of people, including their reactions and attitudes to one another

hyperbole a form of exaggeration used in literature

imagery visually descriptive or figurative language, which conveys ideas or emotions

internal structure the way the story in a piece of literature is organized in order to develop the narrative

irony a technique where what is said or presented differs from what is actually meant

lighting rig a bar or set of bars from which stage lanterns and special lights are suspended; they may be concealed but are often exposed

metaphorical from 'metaphor', a comparison of one thing, idea or action to another for effect and to suggest a similarity

monologue a long speech given by a single actor with no interruption from other characters

monosyllable a word made up of a single part, such as 'dead' or 'thing'

naturalism a style of theatre that attempts to mirror real life

non-verbal communication that occurs when people express their feelings or attitudes without words, using facial expressions, gestures and/or movements

pastoral literature literature that presents an idealized image of country life, lived among the fields; it often involves characters retreating into the world of the countryside and then returning to their everyday lives

penance (in the Christian church) an act or deed done to make amends for a 'sin' committed

persona the part that a character or the narrator adopts in a literary work

physical theatre a style of theatre that places as much emphasis on the movement of the actors as on the delivery of text

playing age the age range that an actor is capable of portraying on stage

polysyllabic a word made up of more than one syllable, e.g. 'blanket' or 'dandelion'

props moveable objects used on stage by the actors

protagonist the main character in a work of drama or fiction

Renaissance literature literature in Europe written between the 14th and 16th centuries

rhetorical question a question that does not anticipate an answer but is used to create an effect

simile a figure of speech that compares one thing to another using the words 'like' or 'as'

story-telling theatre a type of theatre that concentrates on telling a story, such as a fairy tale, myth or legend, using imaginative dramatic devices, such as actors playing multiple roles, puppetry and multi-media presentations

stream of consciousness a style of writing that mirrors a character's continuous and unedited thoughts

sub-plot is related to, but not as important as, the main plot in fiction or drama

symbolic acting as a symbol; something that represents ideas beyond itself, e.g. Adam's fall through the grille might represent Adam and Eve's expulsion from the Garden of Eden

theme a subject or idea that is repeated or developed in a literary work

tone mood or attitude

verbatim theatre a form of theatre created by editing the spoken words or written testimony of real people about a particular event

OXFORD
UNIVERSITY PRESS

Great Clarendon Street, Oxford, OX2 6DP, United Kingdom

Oxford University Press is a department of the University of Oxford.
It furthers the University's objective of excellence in research, scholarship,
and education by publishing worldwide. Oxford is a registered trade mark
of Oxford University Press in the UK and in certain other countries

British Library Cataloguing in Publication Data
Data available

ISBN 978-019-839892-9
Kindle edition ISBN 978-019-839893-6

10 9 8 7 6 5 4 3 2 1

Printed in Great Britain by CPI Group (UK) Ltd., Croydon CR0 4YY

Acknowledgements
Extracts from *DNA* by Dennis Kelly (Oberon, 2008), copyright ©
Dennis Kelly 2008, used by permission of Oberon Books Ltd.

The author and publisher would like to thank the following for
permission to use their photographs:

Cover: © Enigma/Alamy Stock Photo; **p8, p11**: Shutterstock; **p12**:
Arco Images GmbH/Alamy Stock Photo; **p14, 61, 67, 72, 79**: Hull
Truck Theatre Company; **p16, 38, 51, 57, 72**: Robert Workman; **p26**:
Heathcliff O'Malley/REX/Shutterstock; **p29**: REUTERS/Alamy Stock
Photo; **p30**: iStockphoto; **p33**: John Larkin/Alamy Stock Photo; **p45,
69**: © Photostage